Twayne's United States Authors Series

Sylvia E. Bowman, *Editor*

INDIANA UNIVERSITY

Wilbur Daniel Steele

WILBUR DANIEL STEELE

By MARTIN BUCCO

Colorado State University

 198

Twayne Publishers, Inc.   ::   New York

For Edith

Preface

This book is the first full-length introduction to the art, mind, and life of Wilbur Daniel Steele—one of America's master story writers from the mid-1910's to the early 1930's. Today, alas, all of Steele's books—stories, novels, plays—are out of print and difficult to locate. Because of this cloudy state, my critical-analytical discussions of separate works rely to a fair extent on plot outlines. This method, while irksome perhaps to the rare scholar with Steele's whole canon fresh in mind, clarifies for the uninitiated reader the relationship between characters and incidents; also it focuses attention on Steele's two chief literary strategems: the intricate plot and the surprise ending.

Besides stressing Steele's collected stories, this study also describes and assesses his plays and novels, offers new biographical information which illuminates his literature, and throws new light on his development and decline as a professional artist. The first chapter deals with Steele's formative years and early efforts; the next seven discuss in chronological order Steele's seven story collections and attempt to treat each story as an esthetic whole; the last chapter draws general conclusions about the nature and scope of Steele's fiction and assesses his place in American literary history.

Although Wilbur Daniel Steele's nearly two hundred published stories are close to the formula of his day's magazine fiction, his finest work transcends commercialism—often in the nature of artistic skill. Because he valued the traditional short story in the way a Renaissance courtier valued the sonnet, Steele worked within its conventional "frame" while experimenting with a medley of ingenious "internal" alterations. For fifteen years Steele struggled to wed the "newer psychology" to tight plots, melodramatic adventures, jagged coincidences, and surprise endings—and he attained a particular and celebrated kind of perfection. But a world in fashionable flux turned to the "truer" gods of "formless" stream of consciousness and to "journalistic" Naturalism.

To be sure, several of Steele's best stories—among them "The Man Who Saw Through Heaven," "When Hell Froze," and "How

Beautiful with Shoes"—are still reprinted in anthologies and remain masterpieces of their kind; they are classic fusions of the "old" and the "new." But most of Steele's unique creations (off-spring of the earlier Poe, local-color, and O. Henry tradition and the later Anderson-Freudian-Hemingway tradition) are today in literary limbo. When I visited Mr. Steele in Highland Hall Convalescent Hospital, Essex, Connecticut, in the summer of 1966 and outlined my plans for this book, the old gentleman's gray eyes lit up momentarily and he chuckled: "Give it Hell!"

MARTIN BUCCO

Colorado State University

Acknowledgments

I should like to thank Patricia Palmer and Stanford University Library for permission to quote from the Wilbur Daniel Steele Papers, and Harcourt, Brace and World for permission to quote from *Urkey Island* (1926) by Wilbur Daniel Steele.

For additional artifacts and information I owe a special debt to Mr. Steele's son, Peter Steele of Stamford, Connecticut, and to Mr. Steele's sister, Beulah Jenness of Palo Alto, California.

For their aid, information, or permission, I wish to thank Mr. Steele's literary executor, Harold Matson, and the following persons: Lee Barker, Doubleday & Company, Inc.; Mr. and Mrs. Frank Dickinson, Denver; Jane Gould, University of Denver Archives; Paul and Elizabeth Green, Chapel Hill, North Carolina; Janet Guitar, Old Lyme, Connecticut; Ralph Hansen, Stanford University Library; Muriel Steele Hunter, Saint Johns, Newfoundland; Mrs. William Iliff, Denver; Reiko Nukaya, Fort Collins, Colorado; William Peden, University of Missouri; Martin Rist, Iliff School of Theology; May Rathbun, Hamburg, Connecticut; Joseph and Margaret Spada, Essex, Connecticut; Max Wylie, New York City; and, most particularly, my wife Edith.

Finally, for a series of research grants, my thanks go to the Faculty Improvement Committee of Colorado State University; for her careful editing, I wish to thank Sylvia E. Bowman; and for her assistance in reading proof, I thank Elizabeth B. Green, Colorado State University.

Contents

Chronology

1886   Wilbur Daniel Steele born March 17 at Greensboro, North Carolina, to the Reverend Wilbur Fletcher Steele and Rose Wood Steele. (Brother Arthur, b. 1877, and sister Beulah, b. 1880.)

1889   Attends kindergarten in Germany. (Sister Muriel born.)

1892   Family moves to Colorado. (The Reverend Steele is Professor of Bible at the University of Denver until 1923.)

1900   Enters University of Denver Preparatory School.

1903   Enters University of Denver on scholarship.

1907   Receives bachelor of arts degree; enrolls at Boston Museum School of Fine Arts.

1908   Paints in Paris.

1909   Etches in Italy; writes in Provincetown, Massachusetts.

1910   First story, "On the Ebb Tide," in *Success Magazine*.

1913   Marries painter Margaret Thurston and moves to Provincetown.

1914   *Storm* (first novel).

1915   Cofounder of Provincetown Players; "The Yellow Cat" selected for *Best Short Stories*.

1916   Son, Thurston, born; "Down on Their Knees" for *Best Short Stories*.

1917   Travels to Caribbean for *Harper's Magazine*; "Ching, Ching, Chinaman" in *Best Short Stories*.

1918   Son, Peter, born; *Land's End* (first story collection); "The Dark Hour" in *Best Short Stories*.

1919   "For They Know Not What They Do," O. Henry Award (second place).

1920   "Out of Exile" in *Best Short Stories*; "Footfalls," O. Henry Prize Story.

1921   "The Marriage in Kairwan," Special O. Henry Award; "The Shame Dance" in *Best Short Stories*.

1922   Travels to Bermuda, North Africa, the French Riviera, England, Nantucket; "From the Other Side of the South" in *Best Short Stories*; "The Anglo-Saxon," O. Henry Prize Story.

1923   *The Shame Dance* (second story collection); travels in France.

1924   *Isles of the Blest* (second novel); *The Giant's Stair* (play); "What Do You Mean—Americans?", O. Henry Prize Story.

1925   *The Terrible Woman* (plays); *Taboo* (third novel); "When Hell Froze," *Harper's* Prize Story (first place); "The Man Who Saw Through Heaven," O. Henry Award (first-place tie); "Six Dollars" in *Best Short Stories*; winters in Switzerland.

1926   *Urkey Island* (third story collection); "Bubbles," O. Henry Award (first place); "Out of the Wind" in *Best Short Stories*.

1927   *The Man Who Saw Through Heaven* (fourth story collection); winters in Charleston, South Carolina.

1928   *Meat* (fourth novel); winters in Charleston; "Lightning," O. Henry Prize Story.

1929   *Tower of Sand* (fifth story collection); moves to Chapel Hill, North Carolina; "The Silver Sword," O. Henry Prize Story.

1930   *Undertow* (fifth novel); "Conjuh," O. Henry Prize Story.

1931   Margaret Steele dies; "Can't Cross Jordan by Myself," O. Henry Award (first place).

1932   Marries actress Norma Mitchell in London; moves to Hamburg, Connecticut; honorary doctorate, University of Denver; winters in Hollywood.

1933   "How Beautiful with Shoes" in *Best Short Stories*; winters in Hollywood.

1934   *Post Road* on Broadway; winters in New York City.

1935   *Post Road* published; *How Beautiful with Shoes* produced on Broadway; winters in New York City.

1938   *Sound of Rowlocks* (sixth novel); winters in New York City and travels to Europe.

1939   Winters in Hollywood.

1943   Flying trip around South America for *Cosmopolitan*.

1945   *That Girl from Memphis* (seventh novel); *The Best Stories of Wilbur Daniel Steele* (sixth story collection).

1950   *Diamond Wedding* (eighth novel).

1951   *Full Cargo* (seventh story collection).

1952   *Their Town* (ninth novel).

1955   *The Way to the Gold* (tenth novel).

1956   Moves to Old Lyme, Connecticut.
1964   Enters Essex Rest Home, Connecticut.
1965   Enters Highland Hall Convalescent Hospital, Essex.
1967   Norma Steele dies.
1970   Wilbur Daniel Steele dies May 26.

CHAPTER 1

The Suffering Apprentice

B ETWEEN World War I and the great depression, the radiant stories of Wilbur Daniel Steele won so many prizes and admirers that even after Sherwood Anderson and Ernest Hemingway drove melodrama and plot out of vogue, Steele's champions considered him to be still one of the greatest masters of the short-story form. Although Steele's finest work has yet to receive the critical attention it deserves, no history or comprehensive anthology of the American short story ignores his presence. In the tradition of O. Henry, Steele wrote the best "popular" stories of his day, most of them for *Harper's Magazine* and *Pictorial Review.* Between "old-fashioned" writers like Edgar Allen Poe, Nathaniel Hawthorne, Henry James, Jack London, and O. Henry and the "modern" writers like Sherwood Anderson, Ernest Hemingway, Ring Lardner, F. Scott Fitzgerald, and William Faulkner stands Wilbur Daniel Steele, a curious transitional figure. Unlike the rebellious naturalistic impressionism of that end-of-the-century prodigy Stephen Crane, Steele's idiosyncratic Romantic Realism more gracefully, more generously, bridges the "old" and the "new."

I *Strenuous Child*

An age less primed than ours to assert coincidence might call it fate or providence that two of America's distinguished short-story writers were born in the proud but not especially literary city of Greensboro, North Carolina: Wilbur Daniel Steele and William Sydney Porter (O. Henry). What makes their common birthplace more dramatic, however, is the fact that Wilbur Daniel Steele (with his penchant for exploiting life's ironies) won more times than any one else the celebrated annual memorial prize of O. Henry, so that jesting literati began referring to the award as the "Wilbur Daniel Steele Memorial Prize." Four years after William Sydney Porter (1862–1910) left Greensboro to seek fame and fortune, Wilbur Daniel Steele was born—on Saint Patrick's Day, March 17, 1886. This third child of the Reverend Wilbur Fletcher and Rose Wood Steele received his first impressions of life on the campus of a Negro school, Bennett Seminary, where his popular father was principal from 1881 to 1888.[1] Years later, as a master of the story and as a world traveler, Wilbur Daniel Steele readily acknowledged his literary debt to both O. Henry and the Southland.[2]

Unlike O. Henry's southern parents, however, Steele's forebears belonged to the East. Of his son's ancestors, the Reverend Steele wrote: they were "New England folks from away back, many of them being Ministers, Deacons, dignitaries, back to Stephen Hopkins, who was one of the signers of the Compact in Provincetown Harbor, and who had ten years before been one of the F.F.V's [First Families of Virginia] by being a planter in the Jamestown Colony."[3] Before his Mayflower removal, Hopkins joined George Somers' 1609 Bermuda expedition; some three hundred years later, his famous story-writing descendant, seeking raw material, also explored the Caribbean.

Of his living relatives, Steele was very fond of his grandfather, the noted nineteenth-century clergyman and author, the Reverend Daniel Steele (1824–1914). Graduate and tutor of Wesleyan University, Daniel Steele joined the New England Conference of the Methodist Episcopal Church in 1849 and remained in the pastorate until 1862. First he became a professor of ancient languages at Geneseo College in Lima, New York, and then its acting president (1869–71). The next year he became the vice-president of Geneseo's newly emerged Syracuse University. Thereafter he devoted himself to preaching in Massachusetts, to teaching New Testament Greek and other theological courses at Boston University, and to writing books on religion.[4]

His most popular effort—*Binney's Theological Compendium Improved*—he rewrote in collaboration with his father-in-law (Wilbur Daniel Steele's great grandfather), the Reverend Amos Binney (1802–78), a well-known traveling minister and bookseller of New England. The little book (first published by Binney in 1840) sold until 1885—some forty thousand copies in English and thousands more in seven other languages. The ancestor of all the American Binneys was the seventeenth-century Englishman, Captain John Binney of Hull, Massachusetts; and, like his great-great- great- great- great- great-grandfather, Steele, too, felt himself a type of "gentleman" and "fisherman."[5]

Before going to Greensboro's Bennett Seminary in 1881, Wilbur Fletcher Steele (1851–1935) studied at Syracuse University, graduating Phi Beta Kappa with the first class of 1872, the year his father resigned as vice-president. In 1874, Wilbur Fletcher Steele received his Bachelor of Sacred Theology degree from Boston University and married nature- and art-lover Rose Beulah Wood (1851–1931) of Gloversville, New York—"of like worthy New England stock and New York Dutch."[6] A year later, Syracuse awarded him the master of arts degree. The young clergyman—kind, industrious, cheerful—impressed everyone. His first two children were born in Massachusetts—Arthur, in South Yarmouth in 1877, Beulah, at Vineyard Haven in 1880.

Wilbur was three, Arthur twelve, and Beulah nine when the genial clergyman's family briefly returned to Grandfather Steele's home in Milton, Massachusetts. The following year, Rose Steele and her children accompanied Wilbur Fletcher back to Germany where he continued graduate study in the higher criticism. (He received his doctorate from Syracuse University in 1893.) In turn, his youngest child learned German in the kindergarten of Fräulein Froebel, niece of the great educator Friedrich Froebel, who in 1837 had founded the kindergarten system. Interesting parallels appear in the unity of nature, or God, underlying Froebel's theory of education (based on the philosophy of Fichte and Schelling); in Steele's later quest for unity in life; and in the intense unity of his stories. Except for the soup fat and the grating summons *Vilbor*, the child liked the Teutonic school, especially its demand for disciplined self-activity and physical training—qualities conspicuous in the man's best work. Although spindling, Steele was so active and alert that his teacher wondered if every American child was such a *lebhaftes Kind*—such a "strenuous child." Indeed, as man and writer, he bountifully contributed to Theodore Roosevelt's strenuous Americanism.

II *Danny Boy*

From age six to twenty-one—1892 to 1907—Steele continued his academic career in Colorado, where his scholarly father, excelling as leader and teacher, was professor of Bible at the University of Denver until his retirement in 1923. The Bible and the West are two forces in Steele's fiction—the first informs many of his best stories; the second is the subject of his late novels. Only a generation before the Steeles went to Denver, red men had stalked wild animals among the cactus and yucca plants. Even in 1892 buffalo grass surrounded the college on the gopher plain far south of the city of 150,000. In time, a trolley track connected Denver's shaded streets, churches, schools, parks, libraries, museums, and theaters with the comfortable faculty homes at University Park. Resembling a New England Chautauqua assembly, University Park maintained a village atmosphere of cheerful industry and patient study. On Sundays preacher Steele, bicycling to nearby churches, guided the handlebar with one hand and held the Greek New Testament with the other. University founders and members of the University Guild (Mrs. Steele was treasurer) envisioned the institution as the seat of Christian theology and Methodist scholarship in the Far West; and, because of Colorado's clear atmosphere, the university's chief attraction was Chamberlain Observatory—the prototype for Steele's great story, "The Man Who Saw Through Heaven."[7]

With attentive, affectionate parents, the four Steele children—another daughter, Muriel, was born in Germany—led happy lives, their high spirits tempered by "liberal" Methodism. Although the parents fostered conventional American middle-class refinements —in 1919 Steele's mother objected to the designation "snotty ensign" in a story—their attitude toward art displayed few of those Comstockian fears which Steele later dramatized in his novel *Meat*. Stern only when necessary, charitable Dr. Steele usually left the task of meting out Victorian punishments to his dominant wife, sparkling and strong willed. Prevented by poor health from completing her studies at Geneseo College, she nevertheless wrote numerous travel essays and religious articles for Methodist magazines; and she was, as her oratorical husband pointed out, "an omnivorous reader of the best literature, and likewise very appreciative of art."[8]

Customarily resting in bed following evening Bible-reading and prayers (traditionally the explanation for a Protestant's "rich prose" and "scriptural allusion"), she would gather up one or two of the children for storytelling or for serious conversation while her husband studied. Steele recalled this childhood experience in his haunting story "For They Know Not What They Do": like his young protagonist, Wilbur Daniel also entered his mother's room "for the quiet hour of her voice"; and, hearing romantic tales and ancestral legends, "he knew he would have to be a man of men to measure up to that heritage, a man strong, grave, thoughtful, kind with the kindness that never falters, brave with the courage of that dark and massive folk whose blood ran in his veins."[9] To this warm mother-son relationship—and, later, the boy's love for his father seems even greater—Dr. Steele ascribed the phrase "unrestrained intimacy." [10]

Although Steele absorbed permanent values and patterns of behavior from his intelligent middle-class background—fair play, kindness, self-control—his tactful puckishness reacted against University Park's mellow compromise, contented middle way, and genteel correctness. Polite circles held precious little precipitant danger and heroic strenuosity for the theologian's son, who sought high adventure. Trips to Rocky Mountain canyons, peaks, and ghost towns held promise; but Colorado, after all, lacked islands, sailing ships, and "A-rabs." Later, Cape Cod, the Caribbean, and Africa would offer a brand of romantic vagabondia closer to Danny Steele's Tom Sawyer heart; but, meantime, he found some consolation in the adventure of driving the professors' cattle to the high line. In "Sailor! Sailor!" he wrote:

> When I was ten or eleven, folks in Denver still kept cows, and in the summer I used to go out with the South Side herd. It came up the road in the clear dewless mornings, a smoke of dust past the sand pipe, past the university and the professors' houses. There, bareback on my tall horse, I fell in with the other kids on theirs; musically, to the clickety-clock of split hoofs, the yapping of "shep" dogs, and the seven-beat song of the meadowlark, we passed out from beneath the shade of Scholtz's orchard, cool on the road for half a mile, and mounted at the cows' pace the bald rise of the plain toward the grazing under the High Line.[11]

When Steele threatened to run away to sea or to the Spanish-American War, his mother packed him a lunch; and he and Muriel ate it in their sheet tent on the plains. When not preoccupied with the great outdoors, the scholar's son spent far less time studying school texts than collecting football pictures, drawing satiric cartoons (with a high sense of allegory), cracking puns, and devouring Edgar Allen Poe, Walter Scott, Charles Dickens, Robert Louis Stevenson, Mark Twain, and Rudyard Kipling.

Two events shook the adolescent profoundly: the death of his brother in 1897 and the year's absence of his family in 1899. When Dan was eleven, nineteen-year-old Arthur, a senior at the University of Denver, fell from his horse and, severely kicked by its hoofs, died nineteen days later.[12] Like young Christopher Kain in "For They Know Not What They Do," young Danny for some time afterward "saw things in the dark that frightened him";[13] and he began to wonder about religion. Steele's fantastic "Blue Murder," written a quarter of a century later, perhaps stems from some of the author's irrational guilt feelings; or possibly the popular murder story is a disguised explanation, a rational motivation, for what appears as a meaningless accident.

When Dan was thirteen, his family departed for Europe where Dr. Steele did post-doctoral work at Oxford University. For a year, the boy lived with neighbors, the Martins; and, during vacations and on Saturdays, he ran errands in the husband's Denver stock-ticker exchange. Still devoted to cartooning (and with a tolerant father always ready for a good laugh), young Steele cleverly illustrated letters to his family; the first, for example, depicts a tearful boy gazing on a departing trolley: "When thy father and thy mother forsake thee, the Lord will take thee up." His favorite device, however, was the minuscule Brownie, a spindling figure in a variety of precise costumes and humorous positions, designed to counterpoint or emphasize his messages.

When the Steeles returned in 1900 to the red-brick house of books, paintings, and lilacs (2255 South Columbine Street), Dan entered the University of Denver Preparatory School. Dr. Steele did not pressure his son to follow the family calling, but he hoped that Wilbur would commit himself to a profession early in life, develop his talent, earn a respectable income, and help improve the world. Planning a career in journalism, Steele practiced shorthand briefly—but continued drawing steadily. When Herbert Read, then Denver's leading art teacher, judged that perhaps someday Dan would develop authentic artistic capacity, Mrs. Steele asserted: "I know something of art myself, and I know that he already has artistic capacity."[14] Young Steele's intellectual capacity, at least, was obvious, for he easily became the first honor graduate of his school and the recipient of a two-year tuition scholarship to the university's College of Liberal Arts.

III Class Gentleman

From 1903 to 1907 Steele attended the University of Denver. A history and economics major and a mathematics minor, he also took courses in the Bible, biology, chemistry, public speaking, education, English, and German—and he regretted during his later travels that he had not taken more language courses. Although perhaps romantically anti-intellectual, Steele upheld a grade average in the low 90's (89 to 100), while expending his greatest efforts in athletics. He lettered in five sports (track, basketball, football, and tennis) and captained two teams. His Dink Stover vigor also charged the stunts and solemnities of the Sigma Alpha Epsilon fraternity. Reserved in formal settings, the "class gentleman" sang glee-club tenor and occasionally playacted; but, unlike his bearded, balding father who gave impressive temperance lectures, young Steele shrank from any oratorical display, preferring to help by drawing posters and such. The tall, quiet, gray-eyed athlete gained a unique popularity by peopling the coeds' textbooks with his inexhaustible and disarming Brownies. The typically puerile 1907 college yearbook (closer to today's high school annual) testifies to the popularity of "The Great Campus Romance" between Steele and one Margaret Carmen, a vivacious language major: one item notes that Steele had a "cardiac weakness"; another places the pair among the Amor Frasority elect; a third alludes to the pair as Romeo and Juliet; and still another has the temerity to ask: "What metal pleases Margaret Carmen?"[15] Throughout his life, Steele needed one woman close by.

Although he indulged in academic life more readily than most young talents of the Progressive era, Steele (unlike Muriel) never joined the Adelphian Literary Society. On Saturdays, one or two evenings a week, and during vacations, however, he continued his drawing lessons under Herbert Read, who now agreed to his "artistic capacity." (Steele later used this experience in his Denver art story, "Survivor.") Yet two apprenticeship pieces, illustrated mock-epics in the *Kynewisbok* (1904 and 1907), intimate his later gift, almost parodic, for fusing detail and melodramatic action. Both satirical histories employ the language of the King James Bible to record a bit of campus strife. In "Third Chronicles" the elite and valorous "Preps" (Steele was president) utterly vanquish the "inferior" college multitude; and in "The Book of Wilbur Daniel Steele, Son of Wilbur, Called The Prowess of '07," the sophomores of 1907 capture the banner of the freshmen of 1908, deadlock them in football, defeat them in oratory, and overcome them in basketball: "For the sons of 1907 smote them hip and thigh with a grievous smite, and they sought them a place apart where they might die" (52). When Steele was graduated in 1907, the early volumes of Henry James' New York edition meant perhaps as much to him as they meant to most

Americans who regarded O. Henry as America's consummate artist. At any rate, Steele the illustrator had yet to discover Steele the writer.

IV Art Student

So, in the fall of 1907, he settled once again in Grandfather Steele's house and enrolled in the Boston Museum School of Fine Arts. Although Steele looked forward to the tonal modulations of oil painting, director Philip Hale (son of Edward Everett) prescribed more drawing. Among sophisticated easterners, Steele for a time suffered the westerner's proverbial innocence. So hard did he work in the cold studio (after sifting ashes each morning) that he soon decided to drop basketball and sleep nights. Massachusetts was a place for "doing time" and Colorado a place of "light and freedom."[16] In time, Hale increasingly praised his drawings, especially a chalk nude which won first prize in the spring exhibition of the Boston Art Students Exhibition. So tantalizing were Steele's effects by the year's end—later his stories radiated the same quality—that Hale advised study in Paris. When not at his easel, Steele attended church; read Rudyard Kipling and Thomas Carlyle; studied the Impressionists (especially Corot); listened to the Boston Symphony; and, still amorous, managed to visit a girl once a week. Years later Steele acknowledged that the most important thing he acquired at the Boston school was a "wife," whom he married "sometime later."[17] Of Boston's talented and aristocratic Margaret Thurston, young Steele wrote home: "One of the girls from the cast class posed for me in black furs and winter hat."[18] Later Margaret's father-in-law concluded that the artist had looked at the model "once too often."[19]

After a pastoral Colorado summer painting portraits at home (2161 South Josephine Street) and at Read's, Steele traveled to Paris. Touring the city with him before the opening of the famous art schools were his mother and sister Muriel. The Jamesian trio, Mama, Son, and Daughter, fell in with an adventurous and artistic foursome: the noted leftist writer Mary Heaton Vorse, her husband (Mrs. Steele's distant cousin), Brör Nordfeldt (a Swedish etcher), and his fiancée. Although committed to painting portraits of the highest order (two of his portraits were on exhibit in London), Steele prevailed upon the Swede to teach him etching—to give him another skill and to keep his mind active. Six weeks later, at a cost of twenty-six dollars, Steele had learned the craft. Compared to the delicacy of etching miniatures in the streets and lanes of Paris, the massive nudity of painting at the Julien Academy (Frank Norris' old haunt) and the Colorossi so offended Steele's esthetic sensibilities that in January, 1909, he gathered his tools, bid mother and sister adieu, and joined his four friends in Italy.

Already Steele's artistic temperament was moving toward shorter forms of expression—toward art in a small compass. He studied Italian and etched Barga, Siena, Venice, Pistoia, and Florence. Finding Italy and the Italians beautiful subjects, he observed Mediterranean mores and Roman Catholic morality, unconsciously laying the foundation for his later stories dealing with the Portuguese-American fishing folk of Cape Cod. Literary and political discussions at the Pension Jennings Riccioli in Florence fascinated him as the intellectual life back at the University of Denver had not. Still receptive to new modes of artistic expression, the tall youth in steel-rimmed glasses cloistered himself in his room for three days, wrote a story, and showed it to Mary Vorse: she pronounced him a born writer. Back among the Parisians—Steele considered them degenerate—he wavered between writing and etching; occasionally, he slipped away from the academy to a nearby café and wrote what he later described as "pretty awful stuff."[20] But gradually the literary supplanted the pictorial, and Steele's mind was made up. Choosing personal coherence over internal division (Steele's strong sense of unity and of his own limitations again at work), he sold his etching equipment, visited a few London museums, and returned to America with a new artistic goal.

V *Struggling Bohemian*

Instead of westering to Denver with mother and sister, Steele reversed his Adamic homecoming. From Boston the Mayflower scion—his favorite book was Samuel Eliot Morison's *Maritime History of New England*—backtrailed to Provincetown. In spite of Steele's lifelong wanderlust, New England's dramatic coast and rivers gripped him longest. In sandy, maritime Provincetown he boarded at the Vorse home and joined the peninsula's vivid art colony, a loose group of freethinkers who chose to live in an atmosphere where "fish-houses, sail lofts, wharves, chandlers' stores, and structures of the like sort lounged like seasoned critics

at a 'first night,' each with one eye upon the nautical drama of
the harbor and the other upon the hoi-polloi beyond the aisle."[21]

Dedicated to literature of social significance, Mary Vorse
opened Steele's keen eyes to the worldwide plight of the laboring classes—represented in Provincetown by the Portuguese
fisherman. But less concerned than Mary Vorse for actively pro-
moting security, equality, and prosperity for all men, the young
Romantic from the Rockies contemplated the fisherman's twenty-
hour-a-day stoicism: "They used to come in from the dories and
show me their cut hands—the knuckles open and revolting—the
wrists blistered and bleeding—and whimper like dogs."[22]

Out of awe and reverence for human nature *in extremis*—for
these new American pioneers so like his own maritime ancestors—
Steele idealized these fisherfolk, so different ("unabashed in the
face of the romantic")[23] from the staid dwellers of University
Park. The Methodist scholar's son now viewed true religion as
faith in life *as struggle*—and struggle as the way to know God
and to achieve immortality. To Steele, the rugged fisherman openly
displayed qualities common to all human life but ones largely
hidden by societal and technological complexity. Responding to
an inner ideal no matter what the cost, the novitiate willed to
render these classically simple and heroic people into subtly tense
stories, not into simplistic propaganda. A respecter of all experience, however, Steele never blinded himself to the value
of the educated man in a bourgeois order. But on the haunting
Cape, his painter's eye for picturesque atmosphere fused with
his writer's ear for suggestive nuance. Certainly the rich synthesis
of his mature efforts—whatever the setting—evolved from his own
faith in life as struggle, the strenuous literary life notwithstanding.

But only after Steele obediently continued his art studies did his
generous father support his suffering apprenticeship. In the fall
of 1909 Steele attended the Art Students' League in New York.
He roomed temporarily at the Benedick Hotel on Washington
Square with three young men "in the uplift line."[24] In the mornings Steele drew; every afternoon, often far into the night and
early mornings, he wrote. His letters home, weekly assurances of
love and gratitude suffusing a genteel rebellion, state that he
rested on the Sabbath, attended church, drank only black coffee,
rested his eyes; and, for parents who, in the Victorian fashion,
believed that great writers led exemplary lives, he insisted that
he was "not going to the dogs in the Great and Wicked City."[25]
Yet other letters state that "the secret of getting is to keep eternally

at it."[26] He brooded ritualistically over his rejection slips, but he joyed over encouragement from Howard Brubaker, Mary Vorse, and *McClure's* editor Viola Roseboro who liked his unconventional amateurism.

During these relentless New York days of pain and poverty, the literary artist in Steele was born. A story he wrote a decade later, " 'Lost at Sea,' " that characterizes an Urkey Island sculptor, reveals something of the psychology of creativity:

I suppose one would have to be an artist oneself to understand the nature of the beast. Patgon tells me that it is a concrete suffering. There's the sense of incapacity. A man is less than other men. It's bad enough that he is not big enough to do the things he wants; what is infinitely worse is that he hasn't the slightest notion what that thing may be.

Patgon tells me, however, that it is by no means "all hell." On the contrary, there are hours, unheralded, when with as little reason a man is more than other men, his feet on the clouds, his head in the stars.[27]

Steele was indeed starry when *Success Magazine* published a maritime comedy, "On the Ebb Tide," in the summer of 1910 ($75) and a football story, "Gloomy on the Gridiron," that fall ($100). After Sturgis, Walton and Company bought his etching of a Pont Neuf scene for the frontispiece of Alice Raphael's novel *The Fulfillment, McClure's* offered illustration assignments. His teacher at the Art Students' League advised him to drop classes for on-the-job training. But by spring, restless for adventure and writing (he praised the *Autobiography* of Benvenuto Cellini), Steele gained a *McClure's* assignment and senatorial permission to board a United States Navy destroyer seeking derelicts. Unfortunately, the vessel found no derelicts, and Steele wrote no article praising a proud America's world-power navy. But he did absorb literary material from the sailors and assured his anxious mother that, "far from being dissolute, they are much more wholesome than one generally finds."[28]

During the fall of 1910, the year Mark Twain and O. Henry died, Steele worked in Boston as a part-time reporter and illustrator on Joe Chapple's *National Magazine*. Between lowly assignments, he wrote stories (often one a week); rewrote his rejected naval articles; studied the works of Sophocles, Racine, Poe, Kipling, W. W. Jacobs; and visited Mary Vorse for criticism and Margaret Thurston for romance. "I have more stories upon my soul," wrote home the pained youth, "than I can manage to write, and I am managing to write," he naively added, "exactly six times as fast as I did eight months ago."[29] When Chapple assigned Steele the task of dreaming up an aviation story in four days (to go with Arthur Hutchins' cover illustration—drawn first), Steele contrived a piece of aeronautical quackery entitled "The Insurrecto" (published in May, 1911). Steele's New York friends advised him to resign. He did. Renting a cheap room and averaging a nickel a meal, he felt aspirations and creative frenzies equal to the literary hero in Jack London's *Martin Eden* (1909). Steele lived in constant hope that, in the end, his scorching concentration would triumph.

Author of half a dozen pieces of published claptrap, a tougher Steele hitched a schooner ride to Yankee-"Portugee" Provincetown in 1911. Here, under Mary Vorse's wing, the resolute apprentice labored over his prose while Hutchins, Brubaker, and Miss Roseboro offered moral support. Like the gambling fisherman, Steele too, fished—for words. And, like fishing, writing offered freedom and adventure; and it, too, demanded skill, daring, and luck. On the one hand it offered riches; on the other, poverty—or worse!

During this strenuous summer Steele first heard a local coastguard legend which fired his imagination. The result, "White Horse Winter," was published in the prestigious *Atlantic Monthly* (April, 1912). Steele's pride in the anguish the story cost him—"every word coming out of me with a scream"[30]—reinforced his faith in life as struggle, in his ultimate achievement as a writer, and in his contempt for his earlier, facile literary carpentry. The *Atlantic* story dispelled not only his parents' reservations about his writing ability but also Mrs. Thurston's reservations as to his marital eligibility. Helped by his fiancée, Steele bought a ten-dollar suit in which to meet urbane editor Ellery Sedgwick; back in Denver, Dr. Steele judged that his son might soon achieve financial independence and at the same time elevate the standards of human thought and behavior. Minister Steele regarded fiction and poetry as instruments—a kind of "Unholy Writ"—for individual and social improvement.

With his strong faith in American institutions, Steele, as a man of goodwill, sympathized with those nationalistic reformers—not revolutionists—who in 1912 (the high point of prewar socialism) battled against vested interests and for social justice. Through democratic process, Steele believed, many evils and abuses could be abolished. When radical Max Eastman of Columbia University (and later superbohemian Floyd Dell) edited the floundering *Masses,* Steele tentatively supported pacifism and socialism. Along with Mary Vorse, John Reed, Walter Lippmann, Carl Sandburg, Sherwood Anderson, Amy Lowell, Louis Untermeyer, and others, he criticized "old" systems, morals, and prejudices. But Steele's relation to the magazine was peripheral, for his only contribution was a negligible sketch entitled "The Miracle" (January, 1915). After the war, *The Masses* maintained its early line, but it died in 1917 after governmental suppression. By then, Steele and most of its other early writers had long since abandoned it to the American Communist party.

But with still no violent rebellion, Steele in the spring of 1912 returned to avant-garde Greenwich Village as a classless artist. Now unable to "dream up" stories, he explained to family, friends, and editors that, acceptable or unacceptable, "one has to write the stories that come along."[31] Still interested in Zolaesque life—but never committed to pure Naturalism in fiction—Steele could be, for example, at the Authors' Club with Arthur Colton one day and at the Anarchists' Ball with Hutchins Hapgood the next. Because he had no interest in what he considered to be regulation or conventional characters, Steele often felt himself doomed to poverty, to selling stories to literary reviews and cultural magazines for token fees. Since he had little pride in his first six published stories, rejections by lucrative but undistinguished publishers especially piqued him. Finally, he broke into *McClure's* (January, 1913) with a rambling adventure article about big-game photographer Cherry Kearton, "Moving-Picture Machine in the Jungle."

Escaping New York's din, he returned the next summer to the colorful, crazy-combed density of Provincetown where people moved along bay-curved Commercial Street on foot or by horse. This time Steele briefly shared a bohemian twine shed near a pigpen on the Avellar Wharf with another young writer named "Red" Lewis. Perhaps because of his epochal concentration and fantastic patience, Steele (as a former Denver fraternity man) took part in Sinclair Lewis' notorious Mack Sennett roughhouses; but like most shy, kind, gentle persons who came into contact with the electrical magazinist for any length of time, Steele found Lewis hard to endure. While Lewis perpetually insulted everybody with his shrill egocentricity, Steele charmed his circle of close friends with his species of subtle idiocy. With most people, however, Steele could not—or would not—transcend what appeared to be a monkish shyness. Like the narrator of *Storm* (1914), Steele's first novel, the author, too, could say: "for all that I made myself out a roistering swashbuckler, by some inexplicable law of opposites I grew forever more careful, judicious, chary of speech, and deliberate of movement" (61).

Steele passed his nonwriting hours in the milieu of his stories: swimming with the dark children of the Portuguese colony; along the sandspit of scrubby-wooded dunes; in the moorish back country of wild blueberry, plum, cherry, and lilac bushes; and sailing po'gie boats and the *Wilmarto*, a tubby sloop owned by Wilbur, Mary, Arthur, and Tony (Avellar). All that summer Steele wrote and rewrote stories. In the fall he began his first novel in Lebanon, New Hampshire, where he wrote ten hours a day. In the winter, he married Margaret Thurston.[32]

The newlyweds spent summers on Cape Cod and, like most of the other Provincetowners, wintered elsewhere. In 1914, they slummed in Steele's bachelorhood Greenwich Village. Here Margaret, recuperating from an operation, insisted that her husband, now roaming East River docks, not try to pay bills with tailor-made stories. By spring, Margaret was well enough to earn a hundred dollars by illustrating her husband's third *Harper's Magazine* story, "The Younger Twin"; and Steele's reputation as a rising young writer was established.

VI Storm

In 1914, Harper published first novels (essentially romances) by two former Provincetown cronies. For *Our Mr. Wrenn* Sinclair Lewis' patron saints were Charles Dickens, Henry James, and H. G. Wells; Steele's guiding spirits for *Storm* were Robert Louis Stevenson, Joseph Conrad, and Jack London. Novelistic probability, social satire, and mawkish sentimentality characterize the first effort of our first Nobel Prize winner (1930); romantic possibility, individual tragedy, and nostalgic melodrama mark Steele's first sustained flight. Unlike his ingenious stories (but like his lame novels to come), Steele's novel added nothing to the development of the form. The impressionable hero in both these novels of education learns something about life in the school of hard knocks. Willie Wrenn is a tourist; Joe Manta, a sailor. Both read a few books, both suffer romantic love, both (theoretically, at least) become wiser. Both books were generally praised. The reviewer for the Boston *Transcript* pointed out that *Storm* gives the impression that the author "knows intimately" its scenes and people;[33] and the New York *Times* praised young Steele's force and skill, but it also warned prewar Iron Madonnas that it was a man's book, with Zolaesque pages "beyond which many a woman reader will never get, or which, with a shuddering of the heart, she will shut her eyes and skip."[34]

Unlike Lewis' facetiously objective novel of development, *Storm* has an intricate subjective plot, complicated by Steele's interweaving of three genres: sea adventure, mystery yarn, and romantic love. In summary, the sea tale pits stoical Joe Manta against man and nature. Close to a red-blooded Jack London primitive, the inarticulate Portuguese-American fisherman Joe Manta, of Cape Cod, wins over sea and storm, mutinous sailors, victimization by smugglers, and (in a climactic display of masculine combat and cumulative rage in the Raw Meat tradition) over volcanic Jock Crimson, "a monstrous flame of a man" (60), a developed brother of Red Whiskers in Melville's *Billy Budd*.

The love interest begins with an outcast woman's illegitimate daughter and Joe Manta's ponderously comic finger-snapping cousin, a kind of Portuguese-American sequel to *The Scarlet Letter*. From this two-chapter dramatization of love-loyalty between bereft Agnes and atavistic Dedos (first published, slightly altered, as a story entitled "The Handkerchief Lady's Daughter"), the romantic interest shifts to narrator Joe Manta, son of immigrants from the Azores, and to Allie Snow, daughter of Old Harbor's nabob. Although their mutual affection reveals itself against an atmospheric background of sea and local color, Allie's regard for roaring Jock Crimson frustrates Joe Manta's understanding. The mystery plot begins with Agnes' unknown paternity, proceeds to Joe's vagueness about the relationship between Mr. Snow and the jailed smugglers, and finally to his befuddlement at Mr. Snow's choice of Jock Crimson for Allie. Late in the novel, Joe is "somehow" aware that cranky Mr. Snow is also Agnes' father, but only in Allie's lucid but hackneyed hilltop denouement does Joe learn that his brother Manuel is treacherously jealous of Joe and Allie and that Mr. Snow, a bankrupt smuggler, bribed his way out of jail with the thousand dollars that Jock Crimson had paid him for Allie, her loyalty divided between Joe and her father.

In self-consciously dramatizing his ripe confusion, Joe Manta straddles the fence between suspenseful mystery and irritating obscurity. Not only does Steele make his middle-aged cargo cap-

tain withhold easy-to-get information, but ambiguities thrive,
ellipses flourish, pronouns seek antecedents, and names like
Angie, Aggie, and *Allie* jostle one another. Early in the tricky
lines of action, the reader gains small consolation from a narrational conjecture: "Perhaps the very obscurity helped to etch
the scene upon the retina of my memory . . ." (38). Conradian
hindsight presumably guides the speaker, but his reflective shifts
from the turbulent remote to the calm present offer strained literary irony rather than mature reflection on the meaning of dark
things past.

Although presumably reflecting "growth," the uneasy relationship between the narrator's middle-aged English and his youthful Portuguese-Americanisms makes for a highly idiosyncratic
style. Between picturesque vernacular on the one hand—"Eet
ain't Snow, eez eet?"—and subliterary affectation on the other—"I
was conscious of whispering above me and the tentative with-
drawal of my burden of assailants . . ."—there are blocks of wearisome I-verb-complement sentences which urgently but intermi-
nably describe fleeting night scenes perceived by a dune-running
Joe Manta. Lacking the natural flow of, say, Sinclair Lewis' language, Steele's congested style, so suitable for the short story,
discomforts the serious reader who might well feel that not all
of the three hundred and thirty pages of *Storm* are worth the
candle.

Furthermore, Steele's great effort to sustain his hero's boyhood
from the age of ten to twenty-two is unsuccessful. Somewhere in
the middle of the book, Joe's attractive innocence passes over into
unattractive stupidity. Joe's final belief that his gladiatorial brutali-
zation of amoral Jock Crimson was essentially unheroic appears
sensible; but, like all of Joe's appraisals, it too is simply felt; and
his rebirth, therefore, is not really an advance over his boyhood
hatred of the "lust of battle" (49).

The book's qualified happy ending of Joe Manta as a self-made
hero, along with its authentic detail and many realistic situations
in regard to local folklore, superstitions, and fishing lore, indicate
that *Storm* tries to be a serious romance in spite of its popular-
fiction clichés. Particularly Zolaesque is the description of working conditions on a pogi-steamer: "I looked down into the hold.
It was illuminated by half a dozen lanterns, pouring their smoky
radiance over figures that writhed and heaved and stuck forks
into the festering mass—demons in hell, if ever I saw them. It was
a moment before I could realize that these were the forms of

men. Their heads and shoulders were swathed in gunny-bags, upon which fell the rotten rain" (80–81).

But the lack of focus in *Storm* contributes to thematic fuzziness. The narrator's maxims about his ritual passage offer little help. If atmospheric turbulence is viewed as a moral equivalent of human rage, then Steele's microcosmic ships and villages hold latent anarchy. In Manta's often chaotic world, luck guides the destinies of minor figures, while major characters ultimately thrive or suffer in the light of some poetic justice. Manta's early conflicts stem from accident and from his misinterpretation of events. But, since brute strength and cumulative rage alone rescue Allie from marital slavery, the worth of a "big-stick philosophy" is obvious in a society which looks upon physical cowardice as evil and calls such evildoers "Pa Jims."[35] Interestingly enough, the 1914 best seller in biceps-flexing America was *Tarzan of the Apes*, its hero less clothed but not essentially different from Harold Bell Wright's "muscular Christians."

VII *Provincetown Player*

During Steele's 1914 Provincetown summer spent in a hilltop cottage, his stories appeared in *Scribner's Magazine, Atlantic Monthly*, and *Harper's Magazine*. As always, he viewed his published stories with misgivings. His sentimental tall tale entitled "Captain Ulysses G. Dadd, Retired" was for personal "relaxation"; "The Wickedness of Father Veiera" did not go "very far"; and "The Younger Twin" was a "cripple."[36] Of his first twenty-five stories, Steele selected for his first story collection in 1913 only three: "White Horse Winter," "The Yellow Cat," and "'Romance.'"

Since American literature during this period tried to keep abreast of American nationalism, magazines often inflated the reputations of their most talented contributors by declaring them to be the world's finest. *Century Magazine*, for example, now billed only Rudyard Kipling above Wilbur Daniel Steele. Feigning bewilderment at his position, Steele habitually jostled admirers with his melancholy conviction that he ought to be *first*, for story-writing was more difficult for him than for "anybody else in the world."[37] Especially difficult was the winter of 1915, when the Steeles lived in widow Thurston's Brookline. Here, in January, Steele's first son, Thurston, was born. Except for the brightness of this "terrible cunning and adorable" infant, the young writer and doting father, perhaps recalling Thomas Carlyle, found philistine Brookline dark with the "dull worship of Things."[38] In the summer, the Steeles were again on the Cape.

To George Cram Cook's little summer theater, one which altered the course of the American theater, Steele contributed two one-act dramas—*Contemporaries* in 1915 and *Not Smart* in 1916. The first was a product of his social seriousness; the second, of his local-color waggery. Besides the Steeles and Mary Vorse, particularly energetic and talented persons (many of them writers and journalists) happened to be among the Provincetown painters during the 1915 season. In liberal but not lax Provincetown were "Jig" Cook, his wife Susan Glaspell, Hutchins Hapgood, Neith Boyce, William and Marguerite Zorach, Edward J. O'Brien, John Reed, and Max Eastman.

Like Steele, most of these Provincetowners belonged to the prewar younger generation with Victorian childhoods. Spokesmen for this generation were Theodore Dreiser, Edgar Lee Masters, Eugene Debs, Isadora Duncan, and Krafft-Ebing. To Cook's inspirational dream of communal creativity in the form of an experimental theater (like the anticommercial groups in New York, Baltimore, Detroit, and Chicago), the summer Provincetowners responded. Ruggedly independent, Steele broke from the group after a few years, but he did at first draw strength from its tribal ritualism. His collegiate zest for seaboard horseplay returned, but according to Miss Vorse, it hid "a subtle, intricate mind, intensely aware of all that was going on around him, and a gift for words and for situation of the first order."[39]

The spontaneity and spirit of this first troop of adept writers, actors, designers, and stagehands has been documented many times. The first two plays that summer—Neith Boyce's *Constancy* (a witty parody of stormy love between John Reed and Mabel Dodge) and George Cram Cook's and Susan Glaspell's popular *Suppressed Desires* (a satire on fashionable parlor Freudianism) —were performed at Hutchins Hapgood's house: for the first play, the audience, sitting on the porch, viewed the sea as a background; for the second feature, the watchers, turning their chairs around, looked into the wide doorway. By popular demand, these two original plays were repeated that summer in Margaret Steele's fish-house studio at the end of Mary Vorse's wharf.[40] This playhouse—The Wharf Theater—contained fish nets, circus benches, and a lantern-lit stage. The next pair of one-acters were Cook's *Change Your Style* (a comedy about the town's contesting schools of art) and Steele's *Contemporaries* (a well-made episode about the cruel police raids on homeless men who slept in churches during the winter of 1914–15).

Steele's unpublished play—well-adapted to Wharf conditions— takes place late one night after a raid. The setting is a small room in a dim quarter of the city, for lanterns barely illuminate the shadowy stage. Among other voices, a mother bemoans the fact that her young son is involved with evil men who invade churches for diabolical purposes. Finally, when the stagelighting intensifies, the audience discerns that the contemporary discussion is carried on by actors in historical garb. The small room is the office of a Roman centurion in Palestine. The mother, grinding corn, speaks of the leader Jesus who invaded the temple. Thus, through surprise, Steele fuses past and present, ironically equating the trials of early Christianity with those of contemporary radicalism. Both efforts are timeless, and the unspoken name of Frank Tannenbaum (who spent six months in jail for leading men into the churches during the 1914–15 winter depression) becomes a type of contemporary Christus.

Loathing New York City now, Steele in the fall of 1915 bought a rambling house (with a shady yard for Thurston, a barn-studio for Margaret, and a garden for himself) near the old end of Provincetown. His brand of bohemianism was closer to joyful Henri Murger's novel *Scènes de la vie de Bohème* than to melancholy Baudelairism. By the following summer (when he took time off to sail with Captain Marion Perry aboard the *Rose Dorothea*, a Lipton Cup winner), Steele had written his daily six hundred words—stories, experimental film scenarios, and his one-act play *Not Smart*, a domestic comedy that shared the "Freudian" summer with his own *Contemporaries* and other Provincetown plays by John Reed, by Neith Boyce, by Susan Glaspell, by Louise Bryant, and by a new discovery who became one of Steele's closest friends —Eugene O'Neill. The stylized acting and abstract setting of Miss Bryant's *The Game*, O'Neill's *Bound East for Cardiff*, and Steele's *Not Smart* undoubtedly constituted "one of the best" bills the Provincetown ever gave.[41] Although the Provincetown continued after it moved to Greenwich Village the following year, its golden age was over by 1922 when Cook went to Greece and O'Neill went to Broadway.

VIII *Windblown Scribe*

While younger writers like John Dos Passos, E. E. Cummings, and Ernest Hemingway were turning to the war front in January,

1917, Steele sailed to the Lesser Antilles and Demerara. His mission was twofold: to write a pair of travel articles for *Harper's Magazine* and to absorb raw material for future stories. As the writer-protagonist of Steele's second novel, *Isles of the Blest* (1924), puts it:

There are some little islands scattering out from the West Indies that someone has called "the Isles of the Blest." I'm going to find out something about human life. That's one of the places where it begins. It's still sensuous there, and brutal and black. The colors are still raw. The sunlight is still white. The air you breathe is—well, what air is that's come to you across thousands and thousands of miles of blue. I'm going to sink down through all that: all those things are going to drain down through me, like a sieve. And then I'm going to start and write. . . .[42]

For two months Steele observed activities surrounding the ninety-day transfer of the Danish West Indies to the United States. Of Saint Thomas, Saint John, and Santa Cruz in the Virgin Islands, he viewed the first as "languorous and self-contained"; but his ubiquitous native boy, pointing out mere bananas and government houses, punctured his craving for romantic reality and for ironic twists of fate: "I waited to hear of black magic done in the hush of a night out there beyond the hills; of the vast pearl his uncle found last week in Frenchman's Bay, and lost again, overboard; or of the cat blown through the cow-house by the great hurricane last autumn, and found afterward miraculously preserved."[43] Informed by the boy that the capital was lighted electrically, the melancholy traveler muses: "Generations of hard-won culture, a hundred thousand pages of romantic estheticism, lay between us."[44]

Escorted from gay Saint Thomas to silent Saint John by a Dutch agent (a Colonel Roosevelt type and perhaps the prototype of the Dutch *mynheer* in "The Shame Dance"), Steele took in the aura of "calculated dissipation" and "significant disorder"[45]—atmospheric tidbits thematized in his later West Indies stories and reminiscent of Conrad's tropics. From the Cha-Chas ("poor white trash of the Caribbees—16th century French Huguenots who escaped the glory of martyrdom"), Steele directed his attention to English maritime might: "Whatever one may think of Great Britain's colonial policy, her revenue-cutter in the straits was a sight to bring a man's heels together."[46] This remark informs "The

Anglo-Saxon," a story which dramatizes the heredity-environment conflict. Steele described southernmost Santa Cruz as an earthly paradise, a frequent image in his fiction; and, always alert to ironic juxtaposition, he appropriated for fictional purposes the nautical bond he observed between New England and the Caribbean: "For in those hot harbors almost every schooner one sees, white of paint and black of crew, was once black of paint and white of crew, riding the gray seas of the Banks or the Georgias or the Channel."[47] What brought cod to intellectual Boston now brings copra to rank Trinidad, and such a craft is *La Guiablesse*, the strange schooner in the story of the same name.

En route back to Provincetown, Steele tried to imagine the curious sights of Antigua and Dominica—the mud, the natives, the crocodiles—but the collapse of the czarist regime in the March Revolution of 1917 and America's declaration of war against Germany on April 6 intruded too forcefully. Unable to write at sea, he completed his fragmentary *Harper's* articles at home. Compared to current events and his own anti-Kaiser feelings, his pre-war stories—"Half Ghost" in *Harper's* and "Free" in *Century*—seemed trivial. Certainly this was no time to publish a hard-cover version of his Frank Stocktonish *Harper's* serial, "Mr. Timmons Tackles Life."

When Edward J. O'Brien, idealistic Provincetowner and editor of the influential *Best Short Stories of America*, dedicated the 1917 volume to Steele, he wrote the author: "Why did you do it? Confound it, there's nobody else in the running with you any more, not even Mrs. Gerould who is audibly panting."[48] In his first collection two years earlier—containing Steele's "Yellow Cat"— O'Brien lamented the commercial short story. Trying to disengage "the honest good from the meretricious mass," he pointed out that, "here and there in quiet places, usually far from great cities, artists are laboring quietly for a literary ideal, and the leaven of their achievement is becoming more and more impressive every day."[49] Steele and Katherine Fullerton Gerould impressed him most. The next year, 1916, O'Brien again placed the pair at the head of their fellow artists—reprinting Steele's "Down on Their Knees"—and saw great promise in a young writer named Sherwood Anderson.

What especially impressed O'Brien about Steele were his individuated characters, the "deepening substance and the gradual perfecting of his art."[50] The 1917 dedicatory volume pointed out that the American story best revealed "the fresh naïveté of childhood in its discovery of life," but that Steele's stories, in the Great

English line, embodied a new and sophisticated American technique.[51] O'Brien incautiously declared Steele's "Ching, Ching, Chinaman," "White Hands," and "The Woman at Seven Brothers" as the three best stories of 1917 and then predicted their literary permanence. In all, he listed seven of Steele's ten published stories that year as three-star. Steele himself disliked O'Brien's "big three," particularly the reprinted "Ching, Ching, Chinaman." Of his crop that year, Steele considered "A Devil of a Fellow" *least worst*. Rightly, he cited "The White Man," "Eternal Youth" (an academic story about a disillusioned athlete who returns to the womb of alma mater), and "A Man's a Fool"—all earlier stories—as better than most of his 1917 stories.

But the publication in 1917 of "White Hands" and "Ching, Ching, Chinaman" in top-paying *Pictorial Review* began an editorial friendship between Arthur T. Vance and Steele which lasted until the magazine was sold in 1932. During this time and the 1920's this popular women's magazine often lured writers away from *Atlantic Monthly* and *Harper's Magazine*; and it published, for example, Edith Wharton's *Age of Innocence*, Booth Tarkington's *Alice Adams*, as well as work by Carl Sandburg, Gertrude Atherton, and Joseph Conrad. But it was *Harper's Magazine*—designed for "well-to-do readers of catholic tastes"[52] and interested in the living present—that invited Steele to submit one story a month through 1918.

This same year the Society of Arts and Sciences founded the *O. Henry Memorial Award Prize Stories* (1919–   ), which offered two annual awards—$500 for the first and $250 for the second prize stories—as well as reprinting other prize stories. During the next decade Steele was to offer this committee, which favored unified, tightly plotted stories, an embarrassment of riches. The February *Bookman* featured Steele among America's eleven best writers. Steele's photograph shows a suave cosmopolitan: his "camera eyes" gaze seriously through steel-rim glasses, his large mustache (which he habitually teased) accents full lips, and his wide-brimmed fedora angles over his high-collared coat. O'Brien, who wrote the accompanying article, again predicted Steele's literary permanence because of Steele's consummate portrayal of pictorialized action and spiritual conflict. In conclusion, O'Brien likened Steele's sense of human mystery and his rich tragic humor to Thomas Hardy's, but he felt them to be "infinitely more hopeful."[53]

Steele—bored by his winter in Springfield, Massachusetts, and, like other writers, numbed by the war—reconstructed some of his early stories, especially his unusual fictional essay "Dark Hour," and worried about Margaret's pregnancy. After a hard birth, Steele's second and last child, Peter, was born on April 22. In Provincetown for the 1918 season, Steele began putting together a collection of his sea stories for book publication; but the stories dealing with his mythical Urkey Island he saved for a later collection.

Restless by fall and still pondering the war, Steele accepted a three-article assignment from *Cosmopolitan Magazine* as a foreign correspondent attached to the United States Navy, stationed off the coasts of Ireland, England, and France. Three times he rode out of Queenstown on a destroyer escorting convoys into British ports. He fused this experience into "Contact," a nonfiction story (or a highly imaginative article) which confounded the five admiring judges of the 1919 O. Henry Awards. After viewing the sea war with the North Sea fleet, Steele looked at the air war from the Naval Aviation Base in Killingholme and from the bombing group in Dunkirk. From Dover Steele crossed the English Channel in a British destroyer and visited the lines behind Nieuport, describing with Hemingwayesque detachment "a fine morning of long-range bombardment in Dunkirk."[54] Late in October, 1918, the windblown scribe returned to Provincetown, glad to be with his family and to behold a copy of his first collection of short stories.

CHAPTER 2

Land's End

A LTHOUGH *Land's End and Other Stories* (1918) suffered no sensational attention, reviewers noted Steele's unusual talent and especially recommended the collection to sea-lovers casting about for mystery, force, and legend. The New York *Times,* labeling the stories "weird," praised Steele's dramatic economy.[1] Seeing cleverness as no compensation for straining after effects, however, *The Dial* preferred "simpler motives that glowed in a setting of original quality" and argued that strange themes merely emphasized conventional backgrounds.[2] In the pale and provincial light of Joseph T. Lincoln's quaint Cape Cod folks and Down East "cap'n" yarns, we wonder if Steele really did not paint those old shores in such a way as to satisfy a demand for "original" settings.

Based on Steele's shrewd observation and sympathetic understanding of clashing cultures in a melting pot, five of the ten heavily atmospheric *Land's End* stories treat the hardy Portuguese-American fisherfolk who indulge in big talk and bright colors. Like their dark-skinned children, they tend toward credulity, sensitivity, and jealousy. With what Steele sees as art, poetry, and heroism, they ply the deep Atlantic and brood on their little green Cape gardens. After crises on sea or land, the religious fervor of Catholic devotion restores them.

Of Steele's seven story collections, only *Land's End* contains an introduction. Here Steele's strongest early champion, Edward J. O'Brien, asserts that since 1912 the author has followed a course of "uncompromising fidelity to his literary ideals" and that his art "bears all signs of permanence" (ix). After praising Steele's Romantic view of ordinary life, his sense of humor, atmospheric landscapes, brilliant economy, and his powerful use of suggestion and implication, O'Brien concludes: "Almost without exception they represent the best that is being accomplished in America to-day by a literary artist. But Mr. Steele will never be elected to an Academy. Such is the fate of all pioneers" (xiii). Steele's first collection includes the following stories, mostly from *Harper's Magazine*: "Land's End," "The Woman at Seven Brothers," "White Horse Winter," "Down on Their Knees," "The Killer's Son," "A Devil of a Fellow," "The Yellow Cat," "A Man's a Fool," "Ked's Hand," and " ' Romance.' "

I *"Land's End"*

Steele's compound of mystification, irony, and atmosphere in "Land's End" partly redeems its melodramatic plot: the purported long-lost lover who forgoes his worshipping from afar to save his lady from insanity and death. Besides suggestions from the shifting dramatic point of view (subtle and bold hints designed to intensify suspense and dispel implausibility), the denouement offers three improbable surprises: first, the Good Samaritan who comes upon an hysterical woman floundering on a muddy back road, provides care for her in his decaying, wind-swept house, learns from her that she is a mentally ill operatic singer, professes his love for her, and then shocks her back to reality with his double suicide attempt by drowning—this Good Samaritan, Mendal, really is the eminent Dr. Westcountry. Second, Dr. Westcountry, engineer of the hygienic hoax and climactic "suicide," also is the diva's true lost love, the young intern who ten years earlier had begged her to forgo the mad theatrical world. And third, the operatic Mary Farnoe confesses that she began to suspect a week before that the compassionate Mendal was indeed her young worshiper because "there couldn't be two of you."

Disturbing to the slice-of-lifer, these concentrated improbabilities heavily underscore the notion that Mary Farnoe's deathbed indictment of theatrical facade turns out, after all, to be psychotic murmuring. After Westcountry's sham suicide destroys her commitment to the role of the mad singer in *Lucia*, Mary realizes—part of her psychological rebirth—that the curtain of the commonplace has rung down on her grand dramatic gesture played on the operatic stage of atmospheric Land's End, with its symbolic scenery of beckoning bell, eternal ocean, and oblivion. Westcountry's clear-minded playacting and Mary Farnoe's confused role-playing are contrasting idealizations of good and ill that emerge from donning masks and playing parts. Steele's multiple unmaskings at the end reinforce the moral that, since assuming roles is inevitable, the trick is for the masker to distinguish between the role and the real.

II "*The Woman at Seven Brothers*"

Like "Land's End," the next story exhibits Steele's fondness for situations involving mental derangement; but, better than most of his "sick" literature, "The Woman at Seven Brothers" also illustrates Steele's ability to render novel but convincing plots. In this story the reader overhears mentally deranged Ray Johnson recount in a bare style his partly understood, partly delusional, past experience to an unidentified "Sir" in an asylum. After asserting his sanity, the patient chronologically describes his humdrum work as young assistant in the lonely lighthouse of Seven Brothers, his only companions the morbid old lightkeeper and the lightkeeper's young wife; after she breaks the monotony with a series of seductive overtures toward the recoiling yet fascinated Ray Johnson (weak, straitlaced, inexperienced, moody), he is beside himself.

Alone one stormy night after the Feddersons row ashore for a welcome change, his nerves unhinged by the seesaw of detailed influences—normal and abnormal, within and without—the introspective boy yields to hallucinations of sexual enticement and murder, becomes insane, and ends in the asylum, where the *roman,* or outer story, begins. Fortunately, the thick psychopathic atmosphere pervades both story and study admirably; for Ray Johnson's contrary moods, characteristic of mental aberration, contribute also to artistic relief.

III "*White Horse Winter*"

"White Horse Winter" purports to be a tale from Joe Manta's remembered boyhood amid the magic dunes of Cape Cod. As in the novel *Storm,* the nostalgic narrator heightens the atmosphere of his wonder story about a shipwreck and a mysterious white stallion by weaving in his mother's Portuguese folk song: "The herd of the Sea King's White Horses/Comes up on the shore to graze." The great unfettered stallion is a dynamically symbolic backdrop for the shipwrecked Jem Hodges' silent wooing of Joe Manta's older sister. The stallion's supernaturalism is dispelled shortly after the fiery girl challenges her seemingly fearful Anglo-Saxon lover to capture the great white beast.

Out of the climactic fusion of terror, darkness, water, and sand, the stallion responds to Jem's strange whistle and explodes out of the night, whereupon the Englishman confesses that the horse belongs to him and his father, but that, after the shipwreck, he had wished the horse free rather than delivered to a rich American "leddy." The psychical distance between what the ten-year-old "Zhoe" saw and what the older Joe Manta remembers imparts to Steele's composite description of man, woman, and horse an illusion of sandy anarchism settling into mystical unity.

IV "Down on Their Knees"

Similar to the romantic-religious last scene of "White Horse Winter" is the ecstatic finale of "Down on Their Knees" in which Steele dramatizes the centrality of pride as a Christian sin. Like *Moby Dick*'s Ahab, Captain Peter Duarte has only one leg. Old Harbor—once drab and austerely English but now brightly colored and Portuguese—is heir to the fishing captain's general rancor. Rich and proud, Peter Um Perna (Peter One-Leg) is hated by his crew, who agree, however, that their master is a "dog" for knowing the fish (86). On his three vessels or in his white-pillared hill house, Duarte displays no humility or tenderness, especially towards pretty Angel Avellar. Urged by her shrewd washerwoman-grandmother to deliver to the mad Um Perna a clean shore shirt, Angel confronts his niggardly sister Philomena—and then Um Perna himself sadistically taunts her. He declares that he seeks a rich, fair wife—not a poor, dark girl who comes crawling. Begging one of Um Perna's crew (her boy friend Man'el Costa) to "kill the one-leg pig" (94), Angel quickly hardens.

Soon she becomes glitteringly beautiful and contemptuous of Peter's brass-shod peg and russet shoe. By Christmas, her campaign of revenge is undiminished; but Peter, weary after battling the winter sea and relaxed with festive wine of *Menin' Jesus,* not only seeks a truce but drops to his knees before the Angel of his love, almost an allegory of Christian initiation after the failure of self-love. Before family and friends, sobering Peter and vengeful Angel fearlessly challenge each other to consummate a marriage of hate: "Old Harbor will forget many things before it forgets that morning of passion" (105). When Peter goes fishing with angry Man'el (on the wedding day), Angel assumes that her husband cannot stand the sight of her. Philomena laments, however, that Peter endangers himself because Angel cannot stand the sight of *him*.

Angel sees through this tragedy of errors and learns of Peter's brutal compensatory behavior. Realizing now that Peter is essentially a sweet man who has loved her years before, Angel abuses Man'el who has left Peter to drown and pleads with a rescue party at Peak Hill to save her husband. Finding Peter crying in his forecastle, Angel goes down on her knees to him as the sky turns blue. Through Angel's unconditional surrender, Steele dramatizes the other side of the temperamental Latin coin and achieves an expansive happy ending—tragicomic, bittersweet, glowing.

V *"The Killer's Son"*

In "The Killer's Son" Steele's technical and psychological subtlety transforms an old-fashioned melodramatic motif (the establishment of the hero's paternity) into mythic plot (a son's romance-quest for his father). The documented *récit* or inner story of Anthony Brown and his mother unfolds by way of a sympathetic narrator, a Vermont doctor. Some of the events chronicled the doctor has seen; some, he has heard from a crooked-headed man; the rest, he has heard from the mature Anthony. From Anthony's childhood angle of vision, the family doctor reports the youth's frustration, the boy's shadowy recollections of a faraway village, a father, a brother, even a different name. Through oblique selection, the author compels the reader to assume that Mrs. Brown's habitual frenzy—her angry evasions, her destruction of Anthony's toy boat, her fear of storm, her effort to flee from a crooked-headed man—is an outgrowth of her mysterious residence in Vermont.

This strategy of revelation and concealment also makes the reader suppose that the terrified woman is trying to escape the social stigma of a convict's wife and a killer's son. After his mother's death, seventeen-year-old Anthony Brown finds a clue to his identity and stows away on a Portuguese fishing boat out of Boston. At sea, the angry captain threatens to "feex" the stowaway; but there seems to reside in the youth some "high authority, ancient and irrevocable, handed down through generations . . . " (140). The upshot of the boy's strange power is that the captain fishes where the boy casually suggests. On board is a crooked-headed cook, who resolves all incertitude. Anthony

Brown is the son of the killer *Tony Bragana*: "W'en any feeshin' skeeper he take, ever' year, mush feesh, then we call heem 'Killer' " (147). All the Braganas—except Anthony—have died at sea. Always there must be a Bragana to find fish for his people. At his suggested fishing spot, the boy ecstatically screams: "Ah, *Bakalhov!—Miuto!*" (Cod!—Many!). From old Portuguese gossips, the narrator later learns that the boy's inland-born mother was a queer, bad woman for trying to keep a Bragana from his destiny.

Thus through this device of a Jamesian central intelligence in the form of a bewildered but perceptive medical man, Steele ultimately synthesizes his clever disparities. To some readers the writer's exploitation of the ambiguous term "killer" may be little more than a gimmick; but on a higher level the story does convey the machinery of destiny as seen by Portuguese fisherfolk and "underdeveloped" peoples everywhere. Only the fearful alien, represented by Anthony's mother, is out of tune with the great and mysterious forces of nature. By answering the hereditary call of the wild sea, Anthony Brown has found his place in the sun. He will not die a stranger in a strange land.

VI *"A Devil of a Fellow"*

"A Devil of a Fellow" shows two shipwrecked sailors returning home after seven months—only to discover that townspeople presume them dead, including the hero's former sweetheart, married for the past six months to an old storekeeper. A type of handsome sailor who bears little resemblance to Melville's Billy Budd in the beginning, the "spoiled" Portuguese-American fisherman Tony Va Di is a "gay bird"—"a devil of a fellow." Although his love for Mamie Cabral shapes the motivation which finds him below her window on his homecoming night, their discussion strains to establish the series of improbabilities necessary for the final effect of innocent surrender. Indeed, Tony's letter to Mamie (written by his "yes man" Stiff Peter) did arrive; but because she had already married Old Henny, Mamie (for no compelling reason) keeps the news of Tony's rescue a secret. Ironically, Old Henny himself, Mamie informs Tony, had drowned a few days ago, having fallen off a wharf. Before Mamie can explain her unfortunate pregnancy, Tony Va Di melodramatically misunderstands and stalks away.

Shifting to Tony's family, the omniscient narrator dramatizes the custom of Portuguese homecoming and Tony's monumental conceit. Returning to Old Henny's house when Mamie's "time" comes, Tony empathizes with her in the framework of a groaning universe. By symbolic dawn, Mamie has given birth to her "sixth monther." The lusty midwife, who hands the infant to the confused Va Di, remarks: "You Old Devil . . . I might o'knowed . . . ." With Billy Buddish innocence, Va Di stammers: "He's— he's-he's a s-stout little bastard" (178). Although Tony experiences no epiphany, the reader is given to understand, didactically but subtly, that in a moral universe the pleasures of manhood bring responsibilities. If in "The Killer's Son" the son seeks his father, in "A Devil of a Fellow" the father finds his son without even trying. In this context of premarital intercourse, the nickname of Tony Va Di's "yes man" is suggestive.

VII "The Yellow Cat"

Included in dozens of story anthologies—including Edward J. O'Brien's *Fifty Best American Stories, 1915–1939*—"The Yellow Cat" combines two types of Poe tales: terror and ratiocination. Like the atmosphere of Poe's "The Black Cat," Steele's masterpiece dispels fear, mystery, and foreboding; and, like Poe's Auguste Dupin tales, "The Yellow Cat" depends on a trail of clues, a structure of circumstantial evidence, that leads to the truth. Following his conversational preamble on the philosophy of abandoned ships, the seaman-narrator Ridgeway reconstructs from memory a personal experience—based on the "detective" pattern of predicament, crisis, recovery, and explanation.

Aboard an abandoned ship just reclaimed, the narrator learns from the shaking, hard-drinking survivor McCord that the dead captain's fanatical log book reveals that he and his crew had an irrational fear of their Chinese cook (poison food, evil eye) and that in self-defense the cook stole their revolvers and killed them. The death of his mate on the topmast on a calm day and his reading of the log convince McCord that the Chinaman, also murdered by the crew, has come back in the form of a yellow cat to haunt the ship.

Hearing McCord's account of the long, terrifying voyage home with the transmigrated soul on board, even the skeptical Ridgeway—in this atmosphere of flickering candlelight and dead men's liquor—is disconcerted. Then, amid eerie sights and sounds, both men hear "the dying rumor of a ripple, somewhere in the outside darkness, as though an object had been let into the water with extreme care" (203). Pursuing a yellow cat, McCord follows it up the mast where, in the pursed sails, he discovers kittens, slippers, a brace of revolvers, a kimono, and a soiled apron— testimony that, during the voyage home, the frightened cook hid there, coming down at night to drink the cat's water, the shadow of the Chinaman's pigtail throwing itself across the ship like a gigantic cat's tail. Furthermore, the recent sound of the "ripple" was the "poor cuss'" escaping over the side, an act which gains McCord's and Ridgeway's sympathy. Another sea mystery dissolves, for obviously McCord's inexperienced mate, lashed by the sails, fell accidentally. The story is much too ingenious.

VIII   "A Man's a Fool"

The form of "A Man's a Fool" is confessional, and the title is John Prada's refrain. Instead of saving his money for their return to the Azores (where he and his younger brother Raphael plan to buy a fishing boat), the sex-starved older John—like a fool—sends to Lisbon for a wife. Unfortunately, his mate is Wild Mary Cabral, a tantalizing slut: "Sometimes she get me so I didn't care for a couple of days at a time if the house and the boat and my brother and the whole world even should go to hell" (219). But to his disgrace, Mrs. Prada publicly flirts and swears. Inevitably, the angelic Raphael falls prey to Mary's seductions.

Taunted by Mary's declaration that Raphael is the "better man," John—like a fool—takes Raphael out on a stormy sea and challenges him not to "cry out" in fear. Finally, the falling boom breaks Raphael's back. When John Prada returns home with his brother's body, a neighbor woman weeps, for her husband and Mary have run away: "By and by I turn around and I come into the front room and I set down in a chair beside my brother where he laid on the sofa. And after I set there a spell I begin to laugh. And I laugh and I laugh . . ." (218). Careful preparation—neighbor Lopez' talk with Mary, his hovering near the house, his chastising John for letting Mary "go run around" after Raphael—makes the ironic ending convincing. Although melodramatic, the storm scene serves an important function, as does the subtle foreshadowing of the deep-rooted conflict between the trim Azoreans and the "dirty" Lisbons.

IX   *"Ked's Hand"*

The suffocating atmosphere of "Ked's Hand" symbolizes the degeneration of a zombielike family who haunts the fog-en-shrouded reaches of a sandy peninsula off the New England coast. Without enlisting the witch-curse or outer-space human-oids, the narrator matter-of-factly explains: "Inbreeding did it, they say; that is all, and that is enough" (219). The general tension between the Keds and the mainland folks intensifies as Marcia More watches her talented Gypsy husband (The New Man) turn from the others during a moon-eclipse picnic on the "thumb" of Ked's Hand and impale an "unfeeling" crab. Later that night Marcia, lost while roaming the moors alone, happens upon old Godsend Ked who is firing his shotgun over the water, trying since "yeste'day" to bring up the body of a drowned son.

Marcia next witnesses Godsend's surrealistic death as he stum-bles over his own fence with his loaded shotgun, and then she sees in the seaside House of Usher the Ked family, including a younger version of Godsend and—her husband's ghostly double: "The people there in the flesh were neither strong nor beautiful. It was hard to say how many there were. Like the colorless things on the under side of a field-stone, they sought shadow, inhabiting corners, crowding in obscurity, careless of contact. Twitching, they made no sound. The head of a very old woman was to be seen, and beside the head of a baby, both of them toothless, bald, the skin drawn taut over the framework gleaming in the high-lights; oddly identical heads, staring fixedly in the same direction" (265).

The Gothicism of incestuous degeneration reaches its zenith—or nadir—when the crazy crone murmurs of how her shipwrecked grandfather Abner Ked ate Martin Ked's leg. Fleeing into the night, Marcia runs into her husband—"the drowned son"—whose heart beats as one with the Keds', his whole being in the clutch of heredity and environment. As if to dramatize the notion that will, luck, faith, and help can conquer blood and place, Marcia's husband grows more animated in the launch back to the main-land. Content to end his expressionistic story with the husband's apparent escape from this maritime wasteland, Steele intimates nothing about the pair's progeny or about the husband's possible reversion. By not carrying the conflict between the eternal and the American Adam to conclusion, the story suggests hope.

X " 'Romance' "

" 'Romance,' " a slight five-scene O. Henryish narrative of defi-
nition, is linked by shifting points of view; the scenes illustrate
the theme of a greener elsewhere. To a young reporter covering
the Boston waterfront, *Romance* is the coming back to port of
a storm-tossed schooner, "luminous, unhurried, like a rosy argosy
returning" (277). Aboard this modern argosy, middle-aged widower Justin Jason, suffering springtime's inscrutability, gleans
from his two sons that *Romance* is "excitement," or "a movin'
pitcher," or "going around a lot"; the ship's cook tries: "—Dance
tunes, yes. And women in soft gowns dancing to them. You can
see them passing this way and that and hear their voices through
green fronds. Or a cab through the Park, or through a crowded
street, bumping just a little when you come to the car-tracks. Or
a fire in the grate when you come home. Or clean, new money
counted right and pushed through the wicket. Or the Head
coming into the cage with his hand stretched out—and nothing the
matter with your books. Nothing the matter with your books"
(283).

To a lonesome girl in a photoplayhouse, *Romance* is the image
of a laughing Adriatic fisherman holding out a big fish; but, when
the flesh-and-blood fisherman next to her—Jason—strikes up a
conversation, she faints with fear. Improbably, a policeman,
assuming that they are together, hails a cab for the pair. Through
the ground-floor window of the girl's boardinghouse, Jason ob-
serves *Romance*—men and women laughing and singing; but the
girl, entering alone, views it all as "nasty respectable."

The fourth scene links with the first: one of the festive boarders
is the young reporter, fired by his unpoetic editor for writing
subjective reportage. The last scene—an epilogue—links with the
second: back on his schooner, the brooding Jason retires, while
the cook muses on the fact that, of course, his captain did not
find *Romance*, but that he might—*"to-morrow or yesterday. It's
not here, you know; it's over there—where the other fellow is"*
(304). Thus the cook's terminal skepticism straightens the record
and, through contrast, heightens the notion of *Romance*, identified with a mechanical plot and wooden characters.

XI *Method*

Although commended, *Land's End* did not make the impact on
American literature that Sherwood Anderson's *Winesburg, Ohio*

made in 1919. While middle- and highbrows escaped the Volstead Act and the Red Scare by reading W. Somerset Maugham's *The Moon and Sixpence* on their cruises to the South Seas, Steele wintered in Bermuda in a cottage among wild grapes, hibiscus, and bougainvillea. "For They Know Not What They Do" won the 1919 second-place O. Henry Award back in New York, but Steele excused himself from attending the ceremony and waited among the banana trees for stories to "happen to make themselves up . . . ."[3]

Aspiring writers, now reading Steele's "classic" examples of short-story form in anthologies and textbooks, sought his advice; but the author doggedly pleaded ignorance. Not knowing himself how he wrote, how could he help another? He explained to one anthologist: "I'm sorry to say that the question you have put to me—as to the genesis and development of my stories—is one which I have never been able to answer. Almost invariably they are made out of whole cloth, so to say, and once the thing has gotten itself together in my head the preceding stages seem in some automatic way to be wiped from my memory. And that's all I can tell you."[4]

In 1910, Steele found the works of Robert Louis Stevenson "full of little dissertations in the art of literature," and he believed that the Scotsman "knew more about the English style and knew better how to impart his knowledge than any other of the last long line."[5] But, in 1919, Steele ventured to write his sister Muriel that "the only way to learn to write is to write and write and write and write. After you have writ and writ and writ, get somebody that thinks he knows to tell you why it is bad."[6] For another aspiring writer in the family, his sister Beulah, Steele suggested as models stories by Kipling, O. Henry, Anton Chekhov, Guy de Maupassant, John Galsworthy, and Aleksandr Kuprin.[7] This information allows the student of literary influences to add, say, Kipling's "suggestion," O. Henry's "surprise," Chekhov's "grimness" to what he detects in Steele as Stevenson's "vigor," Poe's "horror," Hawthorne's "allegory," and so forth.

In short, Steele knew his English literature. Unable, however, to find unique patterns in contemporary magazine stories, he stopped reading them—believing that even his own stories were snow on the desert's face. Although literature embraces a more elaborate symbolism than painting, Steele suggested (perhaps because of his art training) that, before writing her story, Muriel visualize a few scenes which would "carry the meat of the whole thing." He advised her to keep faith with her characters, but he skeptically added that only a "minute number" of writers have anything worth writing about.[8]

Like Joe Manta of "White Horse Winter," Steele might claim his "reasonings too diaphanous for a logical answer" (78); but he nevertheless had a methodology. Where religious Methodism did not possess him, literary methodism did. "The whole thing is that your brain works hardest unbeknownst," says the narrator in "The Thinker": "You'll never realize that you've been thinking a thing out till the business is done and the answer jumps at you."[9] While awaiting the afflatus, Steele lived in a psychological bubble. Seldom speaking, he walked, sat, and teased his mustache. The Reverend Steele interpreted his son's early absorption with a chess board as a period of concentration on characters and events in a story; moving the pieces at intervals, he kept them in sight and lined up in accordance with "some timetable for the gradual unveiling of his different features."[10] Perhaps a statement in Steele's "Arab Stuff" best describes what happens next: "a mental clash, a kaleidoscopic tumbling into symmetry of things sharp-edged and crystalline."[11]

As in the case of Stevenson, Conrad, and many others, writing for Steele continued to be agony—this business of cutting the story from the cloth of one's dream, "the muck and sweat and damnation of its actual getting together in ink."[12] Composing a sentence was like climbing a "mountain range."[13] As "maker" or fully conscious craftsman (at the time of making), Steele literally *etched* his manuscripts with a steel pen—three hundred minuscule words in longhand every morning, each story taking between four and six weeks to complete. Daily, the writer transcribed his lilliputian lines on a typewriter. After the last installment, Steele condensed the typescript, painfully cutting his little organism down to the prescribed magazine length and eliminating all extrinsic factors. Through his power of suggestion, indirection, and impression, he turned short-story limitations into assets. His method defines the contemporary human condition in terms of dramatic irony rather than through literal amplitude.

XII *Form*

Regarding his dramatic—often theatrically melodramatic— stories as fourth or fifth acts, Steele mastered the technique of simultaneously unfolding past and present. Steele's method resembles that of his great lawyer Buchanan Gowd in "Crocuses": "He wrote the legend around those pictures and bound that triangle together with documentary circumstances, with witnesses in the flesh produced as out of the void by magic passes of his hand, with attested hints where hints would tell, with certified silences where silences damned."[14] Within a self-consistent intellectual order, the tight past-present mixture finally fuses into surprise, the "simple turn," the shock of recognition which perhaps defies "outside" probability, but releases a higher meaning—always delightful, often profound—of all that has transpired. Says the hero of "Land's End": "Truth is *denouement*—or it is nothing" (25).

Matching Stephen Dedalus' artistic notions of beauty, wholeness and harmony, in James Joyce's *A Portrait of the Artist as a Young Man*, the Steele story also resembles the Renaissance *tondo*, a small circular canvas evoking an atmosphere of heightened reality. But Steele claimed to see his picture stories as "rectilinear."[15] The method of fitting or framing condensed life into a predetermined pattern assumes total responsibility on the part of the author. Fighting against obscurity, Steele hoped to endow his stories with sinewy but poetic strength by clearly revealing what is not stated. Besides demanding the reader's attention, Steele imposes on him the obligation to *think*. Where a Steele story gives the illusion of formal, tyrannically selected events, beyond the surface of life, a Sherwood Anderson story tale offers the illusion of casual, episodic acts, close or just below life's surface. Both heavily artificial, each kind of narrative provides its species of truth. Steele never quarreled with the "new" story. Besides the stream-of-consciousness technique, there was room for much more—"for dreaming, romance, for adventure, for realism. Literature can have as many forms as life."[16]

Because Steele's habitual expression was ironic—tight, tense, oblique—language adequate for the task of full revelation required a high order of wit. He tried for echoes in his intentionally rough sentences and phrases, units held together by implied rather than by syntactical logic. His compression and restraint remind one, at times, of John Donne's esoteric knottiness or of Robert Browning's synecdochic monologues. The description of the hero's speech in "Land's End" also stands for Steele's non-Attic literary style: "He began to speak with a painful deliberation, holding himself in hand, making each word count as a separate thing, hammering, hammering" (23). The exact diction of Steele's long and complex, or short and simple, sentences or phrases contributes to an over-all effect of Metaphysical intellectuality, calmly ingenious, moving hand in hand with baroque sensuousness, copiously pictorial. Despite the density of Steele's peculiar rhetoric, each story ultimately achieves buoyant clarity.

XIII *Globe-Trotter*

For a year and a half—from the fall of 1920 to the spring of 1922—the Steeles lived in Africa and Europe. An admirer of T. E. Lawrence, Steele in Africa continued to write stories and articles for *Harper's Magazine*. *Best Stories*, which dedicated its 1920 volume to Sherwood Anderson, reprinted Steele's "Out of Exile." That year Steele's famous "Footfalls" was an O. Henry Prize Story, as was F. Scott Fitzgerald's "Camel's Back." Steele, admitting that his "short-story mind" did not move "novel-wise,"[17] nevertheless groped and blundered into his unfinished European novel, "Down Stream."

As a commuter in Barbary (out of Marsa Plange, Tunisia), Steele learned Arabic and absorbed raw material. He slept to the music of goatskin tambourines, hobnobbed with Islamic aristocrats, and recorded in strong rhythm and colorful adjectives his impressions of Sidi bou Said and of a world out of the Old Testament and *The Thousand Nights and a Night*: camels, mosques, fezzes, pomegranates, "chiaroscuro compositions . . . framed to order for the etcher's acid and plate."[18] Later he and his family shifted to the "God-forsaken fairyland of the Aurès of eastern Algeria"[19] and to damp Tunis.

Even with Steele's more than a hundred published stories and his four North African articles—"Commuters in Barbary," "The Fourth Pillar," "The Mendenine Road," and "In the Mountains of the Desert"—he had no illusions about his fame. Back in Oxford and Cannes too many well-intentioned persons asked under what name he wrote. But, for 1921, *Best Stories* reprinted "The Shame Dance," and the O. Henry Committee, praising several of his stories, reprinted "The Marriage in Kairwan." Because of Steele's general excellence as a story writer in 1919, 1920, and 1921, the committee voted him a special award ($500). As usual, Steele accepted the prize, but he excused himself from the O. Henry Memorial Dinner.

During Steele's year and a half abroad, Provincetown and the rest of the country changed. In the spring of 1922 he returned to a time of great license in manners and morals—the era of "Flaming

Youth" and Prohibition. Steele rented a hill house, buried his unfinished novel, and settled down with his gout to write stories. A parade of people, however, disturbed his routine and equilibrium. Although Steele lost faith in his destiny as a movie magnate, "Ching, Ching, Chinaman" sold to Preferred Pictures for twenty thousand dollars. Ironically, he felt that his stories were "bound to go sometime—in the dim future"; but little did he anticipate television.

While Greensboro claimed him along with O. Henry, Steele supposed that "one reader in 10,000 has ever heard my name."[20] *Best Stories* reprinted "From the Other Side of the South" for 1922 and the O. Henry Prize Story was "The Anglo-Saxon," but Steele's royalty from Harper's for that year was $5.33. After years of refusing, Steele finally spoke at the O. Henry Memorial Dinner on March 20, 1923. During the wild Provincetown summer which followed, the Steeles lamented that sea city's lost golden age and decided that it was no longer a place to rear children. Meanwhile, the writer composed and wondered about his second collection of stories.

CHAPTER 3

The Shame Dance

R EVIEWERS praised *The Shame Dance and Other Stories*
(1923) as a fascinating and vivid collection of twelve unconventional tales. Set mainly in remote and exotic places—the South
Seas, the Caribbean, Algeria, Arabia—each story combines Impres-
sionistic romance with toothy Realism. Each story ends, declared
the Boston *Transcript*, with a "stinging whip-crack."[1] Reviewers
again lauded Steele's genius for evoking atmosphere, not only
of the ocean this time, but also of the jungle and the desert.
While the *Literary Review* recognized the "deft touch and the
assuredness of a master narrator,"[2] the Detroit *News* went so far
as to pronounce Steele's stories "unexcelled by those of any other
living writer."[3]

Although the Springfield *Republican* and the New York *Times*
joined the critical rhapsody, the first suggested "a want of straight-
forwardness,"[4] and the second suggested that Steele's "stirring"
themes, "marvelous" eye, and "barbarous" atmosphere did not add
up to Joseph Conrad's "high philosophy of life."[5] Besides the title
story, *The Shame Dance* contains: "The White Man," "*La Guiablesse*," "Both Judge and Jury," "Always Summer," "At-Two-in-
the Bush," "The Anglo-Saxon," "The Marriage in Kairwan," " 'He
That Hideth His Secret,' " "From the Other Side of the South,"
" 'Arab Stuff,' " and "The Man Who Sat." Ten of these stories first
appeared in *Harper's Magazine;* two, in *Pictorial Review*.

I "The Shame Dance"

"The Shame Dance" purports to be "a story of New York" (1)
written out of the Maughamesque experience of a South Seas
trading-schooner captain. Through masterful indirection, the detached but curious Captain Dole reveals the bloody crimes of
Signet, an "unpleasantly complex" (2) guttersnipe and Broadway

visionary who flees the lush island of Taai with his princess. Brilliant scenes of Signet's motivation and tactful afterviews of tropical homicide make the deaths of the dancer's three protectors and the island's devious *mynheer* credible.

Less convincing is the latter-day climax. Here the narrator reports on his chance encounter with an American railway telegrapher in a Honolulu bar. Hearing stale jazz ("Paragon Park"), the tourist bemoans the Polynesian cultural lag—and then launches into a bizarre winter's tale of how one night back in Colorado "some kind of nigger" (33) came into the waiting room of his prairie depot and did a remarkable "Paragon Park" shimmie —whereupon the white bum with her smashed the record.

Only slightly less strained is the denouement. Here Captain Dole explains that much later he ran into the Broadway guttersnipe in the Marquesas. As it turns out, Signet's royal wife learned to shimmie years before on a Papeete steamer full of hula-watching tourists. Amid a tropical paradise, Signet still ponders: "Something that'll go big in the city. Big!" (38). Ironically, the writer has fulfilled the demands of the marketplace: Signet's obsessive seriocomic vision makes this Polynesian adventure a story of New York.

II *"The White Man"*

Like Conrad's *Heart of Darkness*, "The White Man" dramatizes the degeneration of Nordics in the tropics. But for the grace of civilization's checks, Steele suggests, the power of blackness would dominate all but the greatest saints. With mere "west-of-Canada sinlessness" (39), the young subaltern Pauling despises his boss, Clymer, who—between bouts of bat-phobia, drinking, and weeping—manages a lucrative Canadian-owned cocoa estate in British Guiana. Whereas Conrad's Mr. Kurtz once believed in the sacred mission of the superior white race, Steele's innocent Pauling matter-of-factly accepts commercial exploitation, the brotherhood of man, and the purity of God's creation. An Adamic moralist, he busies himself blasting evil snakes from the Edenic jungle.

After the degenerate Clymer succumbs to the suffocating atmosphere of immobilized horror, his proud assistant suffers fever sickness. Shaken by his recall of a nightmarish unconscious and unchecked by his civilized contempt for Clymer, Pauling soon begins to fall from innocence. First, the naturalistic beast in Pauling springs on a young native girl. Then, in a rage of primal jealousy, Pauling kills his house boy. Although up to this point the story *seems* to unfold from an omniscient point of view, the denouement surprisingly comes from a white man, perhaps a soldier, Pauling's guest. Between the lines of the guest's description of hard-drinking Pauling, the reader understands that a few years have passed. Now, like Clymer, Pauling, too, is bereft of illusions; he is driven by instinctual lusts and is one with the rank decay and slithering snakes. In the black pit of his spiritual isolation, Pauling weeps. The helpless presence of the anonymous guest suggests Pauling's lost innocence and the eternal cycle of illusion-reality, innocence-knowledge, health-degeneration.

III "La Guiablesse"

The grim title "*La Guiablesse*" comes from the voodoo "devil woman." Captain "Bigboy" Johnson believes that *La Guiablesse* possesses his trim white Caribbean schooner. Betrayed by his wife in the United States, Johnson plies his trade in all the islands—except Dominica. His fruitless efforts to land there make him believe in his crew's "jungle-nigger babble" (73)—that his ship is trying to *kill* him. When, a year later, the fearful, hard-drinking, fevered Johnson learns that his wife waits for him at Dominica, he and his crew put to sea with "a kind of especial pomp and circumstance of mystery, of blind presumption and confidential haste" (87).

Because the three-day voyage to Dominica is rife with reverie and nautical lore, Johnson concludes that the notion of a devil woman is heathen rubbish: "All that has happened has happened to happen" (96). But the schooner will not swing into Dominica; and, in a scuffle with a crew member, Johnson hits his head on the companionway. Gaining consciousness nine minutes later, he discovers that the battered ship rides the right tack landward. On the island he locates his wife—lying in state. A priest tells him that the woman waited on the island for more than a year. Also, Johnson realizes, his wife died during those *nine unconscious minutes* he had suffered on the schooner. This "coincidence" rips the story's rational fabric in spite of Steele's oblique point of view —that of a reliable seaman-narrator who, with great fidelity, intertwines his own eyewitness accounts with the gossip of a shrewd mulatto chandler.

As is typical of so many of his other stories, Steele paints a last picture with such conviction that it overwhelms the climactic improbability: dark, disdainful Johnson continues to ply the islands in his schooner, now bearing the name *La Guiablesse.* Underlying the story's narrative details is a great silent irony: the mulatto chandler has come to think like a white man, while the white captain has come to think like a black man. This racial chiasma is not untimely.

IV   *"Both Judge and Jury"*

Redemptive rather than punitive retribution for crime underlies "Both Judge and Jury," a pragmatic yarn carefully designed to foster the spirit of the law over the letter. With exquisite restraint, the governor of a thriving island in the Lesser Antilles informs a Canadian agent that an earlier agent sent to the island was murdered by a native. Justice was done—the native was hanged. Now the governor tries to persuade the new agent that the fugitive he seeks—Dr. Hyatt Carnes—should not be tried in Canada for a crime of passion which he had committed fifteen years ago. Not only has the fugitive Carnes saved the fever-plagued island from extinction; but, because of his good works, the beautiful island now flourishes. To each of the governor's arguments—even to his allusion to Jean Valjean in Victor Hugo's *Les Misérables*—the Canadian agent simply replies that he is only a *machine*: "I am neither judge nor jury, sir" (113).

Finally, the agent finds his man dying of mountain fever. Satisfied, the agent leaves the island, tacitly letting the governor know that he will keep the governor's secret: that the dead man is not Dr. Hyatt Carnes, but the *first* agent who has remained on the island to help the fugitive—the governor himself. That *two* government agents act as both judge and jury rings untrue, especially in a story which, by its very conception, cannot develop Dr. Hyatt's charisma.

V   *"Always Summer"*

Through vivid juxtaposition, uncanny suggestions, and outrageous coincidence, "Always Summer" points up the paradox that man's survival depends on conflict. Two opening vignettes—the first, a sloop floating a pair of dead men; the second, a view of a solitary beachcomber moving into the "vegetal breath" of the West Indies jungle—tie in with the placid existence of a Dominican lime-planter. Accidentally, the undermanager of a stateside fruit

company in the islands recognizes the planter as a former schoolmate, presumed dead by his wife and presumed an embezzler
by the law. The undermanager's presence threatens the serene
life of the planter's mistress, an exotic native girl.

Convalescing from a typical Steelean fever—protracted and
nightmarish—the undermanager suspects that his disheveled and
abstracted host is overindulging in nostalgia and the "tropic ritualism of drink" (155). Thus the jealous native girl's poisoning
of her restless Nordic lover is accomplished with genuine tact.
Unfortunately, Steele has seen fit not only to kill off the planter
but—incredibly—to make the undermanager's worried wife *also*
the planter's former wife. We can understand why, in the end,
the dizzy undermanager wants only to grasp his unsuspecting
mate and "go north."

VI   *"At Two-in-the-Bush"*

"At Two-in-the-Bush" is a variation on "The Yellow Cat." Both
stories purport to be uncanny experiences of tough-minded, bewildered, inquisitive narrators. Both stories treat the docking of
a "haunted" vessel under the guidance of a solitary half-crazed
seaman. Both stories uncover clues which, in the end, dispel the
mystery of the ship's "ghost." And both dramatize the white
man's fear of other races.

Canby, the narrator of "At Two-in-the-Bush," represents a
large shipping company. The port is the remote Atlantic outpost
of Saint George. The derelict is the cargo steamer *Rose of
England* that has been hit by a German U-boat. Among the
survivors is Tito, "a huge creature of flesh, black as tar, straight
from the Ivory Coast through one generation in the Caribbean
jungle of Dominica . . . a babe in mind, a three-year-old bullock
in muscle, a particularly darksome and gale-rocked ape, one
would say, in matters relating to the opposite sex" (172). By
consolidating extended and sporadic accounts of several survivors,
the narrator solves the riddle of the "ghost" which the black man
has claimed to see during his lonely voyage home.

The "ghost" happens to be the young wife of the ship's dead
captain. Terrified of the roving black man, she had remained
hidden aboard the derelict. Nightly she had stolen food from the
galley; but to divert suspicion of her presence, she had played
on the black man's cultural fears by shifting the position of her
husband's corpse, placing a biscuit in its hand, and spreading

crumbs on its whiskers. Fascinated, the narrator watches as one
of the ship's officers boards the docked ship and teeters back
down the plank toward "Two-in-the-Bush" (the waterfront
saloon) with the dead captain's fatigued wife; later Canby
catches a glimpse of Tito slipping into a dark side street with a
native girl.

VII *"The Anglo-Saxon"*

The color of Islamic bazaars, Arabian weddings, and Moslem
religious rites is wonderfully conveyed—yet highly integrated—
in the strange "Anglo-Saxon," a story which dramatizes the old
question of whether the human career is shaped primarily by
heredity or by *environment*. Suspending his own conviction until
the end, an American consul puts the question to a doctor (environ-
mentalist) and a tinsmith (hereditarian). The "I" narrator simply
reproduces the Consul's story—as told to the trio in a fog-en-
shrouded Newfoundland saloon. The Consul describes his hero,
Captain Abel Diplo, as the archetypal British merchantman—a
tough-minded, industrious Covenanter rather than a Cavalier.

On his first trip to Africa, the young captain grows ill at the
sight of Tunis, and he confesses to the Consul that he remembers
as a child being sick at some play or other featuring camels,
cardboard mosques, and wrinkled mountains. Toward the exotic
and forbidden, his ambivalence results sometimes in loathing,
sometimes in lust. Before his ship docks, the rigid Diplo tongue-
lashes a crew member, Old Perse, for drunkenness, filthiness, and
insolence. With the American and British consuls, Diplo drifts
among the Islamic throng and comments bemusedly on aspects
of the bazaar. When Diplo witnesses an Arabian gentleman call
Old Perse a "pig-father-pig" (212) and spit in his face, he angrily
orders the old drunk and his pet monkey back to the ship. Later
the two consuls come upon Diplo and Perse drinking *bokha* at an
Arabian wedding.

Amid light and dark Arabs, the intoxicated Diplo dons native
garb and lusts after the dancer, a great white Algerian Jewess.
Spitting in the well-meaning British consul's face, Diplo joins a
religious procession; and, during a riot, Old Perse is knifed to
death. The consuls search all night for Diplo and find him the
next morning outside the city gate. Dirty, bloody, waking from
stupor, Diplo recognizes the scenery of the *Bab Kebir*—camels,

cardboard mosques, wrinkled mountains—as the "play" of his childhood and weeps in the American consul's arms.

To the Tinsmith's conclusion that heredity *is* stronger than environment, the Consul adds his denouement: a week later the Consul had learned from an old hag at the city gate that, after many years, her little black monkey returned—the monkey sold to a drunken English sailor (sold along with her sister's yellow-haired, three-year-old son). The old hag now believes that little Abdallah also will return. When the Tinsmith again insists on *heredity* as stronger than environment, the Consul simply points out that in 1917 Captain Abel Diplo was torpedoed off the Galway coast "and went down praying God to save his king" (234). Thus Steele provides a double-surprise ending by exploiting both sides of the argument and giving *environmentalism* the last word.

VIII   *"The Marriage in Kairwan"*

Again the environment-heredity theme infuses Steele's "Marriage in Kairwan," a beautifully rendered story of Islamic life— and death. Ethel Mumford of the 1921 O. Henry Committee referred to the story as caviar—"Beluga Imperial."[6] Restless at home in Tunisia after his French university education, Habib ben Habib seduces a beautiful but "promised" Mohammedan girl and then prophesies: *it is written* that her husband will kill her on her wedding night. Singing the praises of Paris, the romantic exile plans to return there with the girl; but he succumbs to Islam's hothouse atmosphere and his early training.

The careful reader, unsurprised when Habib discovers on his wedding night that the "promised" girl is to be his bride, is rudely but convincingly shocked when the fanatic reverter fulfills his own prophecy by informing the girl's father that his daughter is pregnant. Habib fails to equate his secret love with his sequestered bride because of his preoccupation with the curious task of turning his Arabian beauty's "slumbrous acquiescence" into a Parisienne's romantic flirtation. Suggestions of Habib's fanatic reversion are foreshadowed when the skeptical French garrison officer, "brother" to the turncoat Arab, agrees to help the lovers escape, but maintains that "between a man and a woman in Islam there is no such thing as love" (250).

Also symbolic of Habib's final reversion is a scene in which he (dressed ambivalently in European clothes and tassled *chechia*) is pressed back through the city gates by the flow of reeking

Arabs. In naming things Arabic—*fondouk, haik, souk*—Steele creates the clogged atmosphere which assails Habib himself. At his wedding, Habib views the Algerian Jewess dancer who also appears in "The Anglo-Saxon." Reborn an Arab again, Habib looks upon all women as objects of lust, and he laughs at the "bursting of faith in the virtue of beautiful women" (259). Sorry he could not give his story a Christian ending, Steele consoled his parents: "I am sure I hated, despised and also pitied that man as much as you or anyone else can."[7]

IX   " 'He That Hideth His Secret' "

In the mountains of the Ouled Naïl, the young Algerian of " 'He That Hideth His Secret' " is murdered the morning after his wedding. Promising his grandmother that he will revenge his father, Younez grows up and follows the exiled murderer's son into the ruck of New York City. Here Younez, a rug dealer, saves Moulay's life in city traffic and becomes his friend and roommate. For two years Younez hides his secret, planning to punish Moulay according to the Koran's eye-for-an-eye. The morning after Moulay's wedding feast, however, the contrite Younez returns to the apartment of the newlyweds to identify himself and to wash his hands of the blood-feud. But Moulay, for two years hiding his own knowledge of Younez' true identity, assumes that the "friend" comes for revenge; and, in self-defense, he kills him. As Moulay flees, the narrator quotes the ancient Arabic proverb: "He that hideth his secret attaineth his end" (295).

The narrator, a former American tourist in Barbary, is an "infidel" friend of the two roommates. Besides linking the scenic New York murder with the parallel Algerian murder, the narrator involves himself first as one of Moulay's wedding guests and afterward as Younez' confidant. In another Steelean feat of skill, the narrator's coffee-and-spice reveries transform the small Greenwich Village apartment into the vast spaces of Algeria: Younez' gift of a rug is a "desert," and Moulay's dining suite shines "like a dozen Sahara suns" (271). In the dark doorway hovers the bride, giving the illusion not of a Syrian-American cashier but of a veiled virgin. "Meat! Meat!" exclaims the narrator. "One may grow drunk on meat eaten with the hands" (272).

Later, when the Christian narrator helps convert Younez to Western enlightenment, Steele clinches the irony of the Arab's doom by having his deluded narrator declare: "The God of the man who walks five thousand miles is awake. Allah sleeps" (291).

X   *"From the Other Side of the South"*

"From the Other Side of the South" purports to be an epic of equatorial rivers—a saga of black African warfare. Up to the Ouled Naïl comes a southern caravan, witnessed by a jaded, dogmatic Englishman and the narrator, a romantic, perceptive American. Steele gains esthetic distance by allowing the story proper—the story of the great war—to be recited by his Senegal orator, the grandson of the legendary holy man Djeba. Mecca-bound, Djeba is, according to the Englishman, "black as a chimney pot, solemn as an archbishop, blind as a bat"; but, according to the narrator, "the essential thing was the man's enormous separation" (301).

In epic style, the orator recites the history of Djeba the ancient moribund wanderer: first, the royal-blooded brothers Djeba and Moa defeat a war party from Gandoland, but in the barbarous counterattack, the two are captured, chained, and marched to a great lake where they are bought by a white man and put on a boat. On the other bank of the lake, they are sold separately. Djeba plants maize and cotton, sleeps in a stockade in Djoja, and is regularly whipped. He receives compassion only from the wife of the white headman who has left to fight the northern tribes of Yankis, where Moa is. On the night Djeba escapes to join his brother, he sees the white driver stalk the headman's wife "as the desert hyena slinks slavering after the gazelle" (312). In burning Tlaanta, Djeba finds his dying headman, not Moa. Later he protects the headman's wife by strangling in the dark her evil pursuer. When he later discovers that the pursuer was Moa, he begs to return to the African bush where he accepts Allah and becomes holy.

At this point the American narrator begins to suspect the magnitude of Djeba's expedition. The context of Djeba's story the American has heard before—from his grandmother Peyton in Hancock County! Now, begging money for his pilgrimage to Holy Mecca, the senile black man creakily sings a queer war chant: "John B'own's body lahs amoldin' in the g'ave" (324). The young American sees Atlanta burning and Sherman on the march! Thus what *appears* to be an absurd analogy between a great African war and the American Civil War turns out, in fact, to *be* a story of the Civil War. Steele achieves his uncanny effect through sheer linguistic exploitation.

XI " '*Arab Stuff* "

Steele's Islamic fatalism, as pictured in "The Marriage in Kairwan," rides tandem with American pragmatism in " '*Arab Stuff.*' " To better portray perilous roles in films for the world's "poor, romance-starved, happiness-grasping human hearts" (326), a naïve husband-and-wife acting team comes to North Africa for "Realism." On the terrace of the Saint George Hotel in Algiers, each relates a tale of disillusionment to the narrator, an American petty official. As guests of Sidi Muley Khaf, wife Flo Danger (ex-stenographer) had sought to experience the lusty clutches of the sheikh while her husband Arno Braun (ex-laborer) had tried to invade the sheikh's erotic harem. But, as it had turned out, both sheikh and harem had shattered their illusions about the sons of the desert, musk, and veiled wantons. Under a hot African moon, the actress had no power to "vamp" the trembling sheikh; and, in a room smelling of yesterday's cabbage and occupied by a brass bedstead, the actor had no desire to possess the sheikh's pregnant thirteen-year-old wife.

After leveling a Babbitt-like fusillade at un-American North Africa, Arno turns to his wife; and, in the awed presence of the narrator, they snatch victory from defeat. Taking Hamlet's cue, they optimistically plan to "hold as 'twere the mirror up to nature" and thereby invent a successful satiric film about the fallacious Arabian Nights attitude. On a visit to Si Muley a year later, the narrator learns from an old household gossip that in the family graveyard lie the sheikh's young wife and her serving woman, poisoned by order of the master during the visit of the two Americans. Although Si Muley had "wept behind his hand" while he had entertained his guests, he had had no choice but to obey the law; for his young wife had been alone with the American "for the space of the cooking of an egg" (353). As in Plato, reality for the Moslem is ideal, essence, absolute, light. Thus the flexible but shallow Americans had departed with a sense of Arabic naturalism—but without a sense of Arabic spirit. And the North Africans remain themselves trapped in ignorant rigidity and dark necessity.

XII "*The Man Who Sat*"

Having been seriously injured in a boiler explosion, the chief engineer of a Riviera yacht returns in "The Man Who Sat" from a Cannes hospital to the damaged vessel; and, swathed to mummification, he commits himself to a deck chair. Like the Rock of Gibraltar, John Giles sits in the center of Peg Tyrone's operatic world of perpetual motion and evanescence. After an involved series of love-hate matches (as in "Down on Their Knees"), Giles' immovable nihilism cracks under the irresistible pressure of Peg Tyrone's love stratagems. Cavalierly, the detached narrator explains the improbable attraction of the operatic princess for the seafaring commoner: "There is a perversity in nature which leads the human system, after having dined to repletion on noble foods, rich soups, fat roasts, and perfumed sweets, to crave at the banquet's end a morsel of abomination, such as certain kinds of cheese" (363). But the touring singer flees out of horror, pity, and guilt when her tortured mariner trudges toward her not (as she thinks) on his knees but on his raw stumps! This grotesquerie resolves itself in a slacking surf and in Seaman Tobey's uncertain yet handy contrivance: "Your new legs'll be coming along in a week or so, and then, maybe—" (391).

The story of the stubborn Scotch engineer and the forward Irish singer is retold by a detached narrator (perhaps a former passenger) who faithfully reproduces Seaman Tobey's idiomatic dialogues and descriptions. Tobey's cryptic remarks, surprise-saving ellipses, and one statement in particular (his early indecision about whether he should have directed medical aid to Giles after the explosion or simply allowed him to bleed to death quietly) point to, yet conceal, the jolt of double amputation.

XIII   Isles of the Blest

With five thousand dollars from the movie rights to *The Shame Dance,* Steele bought a Georgian home (*circa* 1770) on billowy Nantucket. Here he walked the moors in watery seclusion and constructed stories. In the fall, the aloof islander whipped his "short-story mind" into starting another novel. (O'Brien dedicated *Best Stories of 1923* to a young experimenter named Ernest Hemingway.) Wintering in Cannes, Steele laboriously wove stories for *Pictorial Review* and worked doggedly on his novel, published the following fall. Like *Storm,* it received plaudits, but no reviewer (however much he admired Steele's

short stories) hailed *Isles of the Blest* (1924) as a major achievement—and rightly so.

Based in part on his 1917 Caribbean tour, Steele's descriptions
of the exotic tropics, as in *The Shame Dance,* almost breathe; but
the larger literary form vitiated Steele's pinpoint concentration.
Dealing with the social institution of marriage, the novel abounds
in platitudinous dialogue, monologal vulgarities, and copious
improbabilities. One reviewer noted that the book strikes "a high
level of style-ish and conscious sensationalism."[8] Unlike *Storm's*
clumsy hero who moves from intimations of romantic love to
romantic love itself, the articulate focal character of *Isles of the
Blest* runs the gamut of sexual love. Writer Robert Ling moves
from romantic sexual love to unromantic sexual love, and then,
after much soul-searching, to a position of realistic sexual love.
As in popular novels of the 1920's, the fleeing lovers' premarital
amours are sympathetically underdistanced, and the unforeseen
occurs with tedious regularity.

Divided into four parts—"The Isles," "The River," "The Plain,"
and "The Island"—time jumps conspicuously, awkwardly, in the
last two parts. Sophisticated New Yorkers Robert Ling and Helen
Jaynes have been living together on a lush Caribbean isle. But,
unlike their Edenic surroundings, their ideal love has faded: "A
love without any grasping or any greed. A relationship that left
each free of the other, to stay, or at will to run away in the wind
of fancy and be alone. An understanding, profound and passionate
and free; never to claim or cling, never to sit up waiting, never to
say, never even to think in secret: 'Is that you? Where have you
been so long?'" (24).

On the same day in which two ships arrive in port—one north-
bound, the other southbound—a cable arrives: Helen's husband
has *divorced* her. After the formality of a hasty wedding, Robert
impulsively maneuvers Helen to the boat for New York and says
that he will follow shortly. In actuality, he takes passage on the
boat bound for British Guiana. The woman on the shadowy deck
with whom he tries to strike up an acquaintance is—Helen! Into
this incongruous situation of double escape comes Harold Hepar,
a naïve and confiding youth from Denver, who is on his way to
manage an oil company in British Guiana. Through the lovers'
regard for Hepar and through his sensational suicide in for-
saken Guiana, the estranged lovers awake to each other's complex
needs—but only after Ling's rough tramp from New York to
Denver and his elaborate domestic misunderstandings. The novel

concludes on another island—middle-class Long Island—with Robert Ling, now a domesticated father and husband, offering a protracted but clear-eyed reappraisal of marital value.

In spite of Steele's heavy-handed rendering of Ling's agonizing literary labors in the Long Island section of the novel, the eternal problem is not that of the developing artist but, again, that of the developing marriage—its glory, shame, and ultimate worth. Out of mutual propinquity, traditionalists build love anew; and, with each successful renewal, love strengthens. This experience gives them courage and confidence in surmounting additional frustrations. Like nothing else, cumulative heroic stoicism in marriage makes for growth; for the last refuge for personal salvation lies in a lasting, intimate relationship between a man and a woman, as in Matthew Arnold's "Dover Beach." Since marriages are made not in heaven but on earth, Steele implies a sense of responsible common destiny.

Unfortunately, Robert Ling's dialogues of the mind with itself are gross. His Ping-Pong oscillations from bitterness to joy seem mechanical, arbitrary, embarrassingly overstated, and his stream-of-consciousness thoughts ring out tractarian generalization. As the hero of *Storm* huffs over sandy dunes, so too does the hero of *Isles of the Blessed* puff over mental mounds. Never downright trivial, never decidedly profound, Ling's (and Steele's) broad obviousness helps blunt his unnatural glibness and punchless raciness.

Although both the New York *Times* and the *Saturday Review of Literature* felt that Steele maintained emotional tension, there is room for doubt. Steele's final view of marriage, at least, does not match the mindless happy endings of popular romance. Indeed, his faith in life as struggle certainly carries over into marriage. Unfortunately, none of the thirty chapters following Chapter I ever approaches the dramatic short-story organization of the narrative, which was published first in *Pictorial Review* (August, 1924) under the title "Marriage."[9]

So dismally did Steele view Harper's promotion of *Isles of the Blest*—"two years of bluggy sweat on the thing, my heart is broken entire"—that he vowed never to send the company another book after his contract expired.[10] During the 1924 summer, however, his one-act mystery, *The Giant's Stair*, was a success at Provincetown. The Steeles spent the winter in Connecticut, a refuge for more and more writers fleeing the metropolis. For 1924 the O. Henry Committee reprinted Steele's "What Do You Mean—

Americans?" In South Norwalk the writer suffered great mental fatigue and anxiety, but he persisted in working on another novel. During the summer of 1925, Steele recuperated under medical care in Nantucket, his novel finished. Walking the moors, he hoped that Harcourt, his new publisher, could sell his effort. Meanwhile, Appleton published a little collection of Steele's Provincetown plays.

XIV   The Terrible Woman

The collection *The Terrible Woman and Other One Act Plays* (1925) contains *The Terrible Woman, The Giant's Stair, Not Smart,* and *Ropes.* The plays are readable, actable, dramatic, well constructed; and, although never as popular as the one-act dramas of O'Neill and Susan Glaspell, they are still performed by amateur groups. Varying in techniques, Steele's plays range from local-color satire to atmospheric mystery. From writing these one-acts, Steele gleaned enough stagecraft to enable him in the 1930's to collaborate on full-length plays for Broadway. In his Introduction to *The Terrible Woman,* George Cram Cook acknowledged Steele's contribution to the Little Theater movement in America and added: "He is one of those rare writers who are rapidly disappearing from this systematic and specialized world, for writing is his vocation and writing in all forms is within his power" (viii).

Of the plays in the collection, two match the general morbidity of Steele's stories, and two are untypically comic. *Not Smart* (1916) is a delightful spoof on parlor radicalism and on the art-colony ideal of free love and the brotherhood of man. In the living room of their rented Cape Cod summer cottage, writer Milo Tate waxes eloquent on the value of uninhibited love and elemental wisdom. In his own home, Mattie, the maid, is a living example—an "earth-woman," she is unaware of Freud, Trotsky, and Imagism. Unfortunately, the Tates always find themselves backsliding into foggy Victorian superstitions. When a friend arrives with a woeful tale of her husband's getting their maid in "trouble," Milo proclaims the experience wonderful for all concerned. But when Mattie herself announces to the group that she is "not smart"—pregnant—wounded Fannie mock-heroically preaches to her husband his own doctrine of harmonious free love. Denying relations with Mattie, Milo prepares to send her to a home for unwed mothers in New York, but by then Mattie's fisherman husband comes to inform her employers that she is "not smart" and must stop working for a spell. Milo now regards the "earth-woman" as a "bone-head."

Ropes—first published in *Harper's Magazine* (January, 1921)—is a lighthouse melodrama. Drearily accepting isolation, the keeper's wife laments the fact that her small daughter must play with alphabet blocks instead of with other children. Later that evening the Inspector, jealous of the woman's marriage to the keeper, gloats when, alone with the wife, he discovers that his early rival has been blind for the past month as a result of a fall. All of the wife's tribulations the Inspector calls "ropes" around her neck. He presses the pretty wife to help him to forget his duty. When the keeper returns, the Inspector mocks the husband's pretending sight by theatrically spelling out with the child's large blocks: KISS ME AGAIN JEN.

The wife passionately responds; and the keeper, sensing something, turns, strikes his head, and falls. Imploring the Inspector to leave, the wife attends to her husband who improbably regains his vision. Suspense shatters when the keeper finally sees the blocks, but new suspense results when the wife blows out the lamp. In atmospheric moonlight, the keeper bellows of his *true blindness*, but then he rationalizes that his wife acted out of selfless heroism. Prompted to speak the truth, however, the wife confesses that momentarily her isolation drove her "crazy wild" to kiss the Inspector. Cursing his fate, the keeper sweeps away the blocks. But in response, his wife, begging him to kiss her, enumerates all of the ropes—mutual experiences of joy and sorrow—which bind them, body and soul, forever.

The Giant's Stair (1924)—first published in the *Appleton Modern Play Series*—melodramatizes the consequences of a past tragedy in a lonely New England mountain farmhouse. *Saturday Review*, likening this play and *Ropes* to O'Neill's mood, described them as "shot through with a curious quality of mystery, horror, and the loneliness of the human soul caught in the grip of the powerful forces of nature."[11] With a Gothic storm, a newfangled telephone, and two sisters (one sane, one demented), Steele creates suspense and terror; and, because of the power of suggestion, a murderer confesses.

In brief, Abbie Weatherburn's mad sister Til rants about the ghosts of giants and about Abbie's vanished husband's walking about in the storm. Sheriff Banes enters the kitchen, discusses the arrival in the district of the prosecuting attorney, and then accuses

Til of murdering her brother-in-law in one of her "horrifying" moods. The sheriff and Til, struggling at the door, break the lock. Every few minutes the telephone rings, and Abbie passes word to the sheriff that neighbors are marking her husband's progress homeward. Abbie's matter-of-fact reports counterpoint Til's haunting refrains. When Weatherburn tries to enter the house, Sheriff Bane tries to bar the door against the ghost, insisting that he did not mean to quarrel and kill him. Hearing his confession, the prosecuting attorney forces himself in, while Til, running off stage, "horrifies" herself in the dark.

The character and personality of the female lead in the play *The Terrible Woman* (1925) are reflected in Martha Hume's spacious, simple, and serene Connecticut home. Actually, this matron, who moves in mysterious ways while she darns socks and who believes that there is a place for everything and that everything should be in its place, plays a relatively small role in the comedy's visible action. Through inverse psychology, attention to details, and precise accommodation, the methodical *Hausfrau* halts her son's and her husband's springtime rebellion.

Martha's young son, regarding his mother in his farewell letter as a "terrible woman" who slave-drives him to bath and chores, has headed for freight cars and cowboy freedom;[12] meanwhile, her restless husband, dreaming of becoming a big, free figure in the world for his soul's sake, has planned an elaborate escape to Europe with a slender, provocative family friend. Cleverly, all-seeing Martha has manipulated the father-son environment step-by-step, making it "easy" for each to overcome obstacles and to arrive in the world proper Christians—down to a five-dollar bill pinned to her son's nightgown tucked neatly into his "secret" bedroll and down to a going-away present in the femme fatale's suitcase, a book entitled *What the Young Bride Should Know.* With the fun of rebellion shriveled, father and son tacitly surrender to the household deity, who, when later asked by her husband if she knows where his pajamas are, replies: "Yes, dear. . . ."

XV Taboo

Taboo (1925) treats the ancient theme of incest—but without the tragic logic of violation. In fact, the *Bookman* assured those "accustomed to the modern sex story" that, in spite of its terrifying moments, there really was nothing censorable in Steele's novel.[13] Indeed, the book—a psychological mystery—is a feat of calculated obscurity. The opening suggests two islanded lovers—he, afraid of snakes; she, of cats—who are strolling romantically through Hidden Forest. The next half-dozen chapters re-create the duo's history. Charming, athletic, and pagan, John Pizarro on the day of his college graduation also witnesses the death in childbirth of his brilliant, rich, beautiful wife, who is several years his senior. Surviving love, marriage, loss, grief, and rebellion, Pizarro finally comes to idolize his daughter—so much so that he later retreats from the business world, preferring her company to that of his associates and women of his own age. Together John and Glenna Pizarro sail to exotic places, drifting from port to port in halcyon idleness.

On the island of the opening chapter, they now entertain architect Henry King, an old family friend who deplores their unorthodox father-daughter relationship. When King, like Glenna, sickens in the presence of a stray cat, Pizarro's delicate suspicions about his daughter's odd phobia and his late wife's friendship with King are roused. After King confesses that he is Glenna's father, the shattered Pizarro flees. Later, unable to abide lovers her own age, twenty-one-year-old Glenna completes college and then seeks Pizarro. Improbably, the erstwhile father burns down his house and sets out with Glenna for exotic ports. Henry King, who had earlier warned of the father-daughter taboo—"the ghost of the damned thing will never be gotten rid of" (160)—fails to stop them. "So with everything against them," points out the last sentence, "they passed out, on their way to heaven and hell . . ." (260).

Thus, *Taboo* is rich in promise, but because Steele focuses on the odor of incest rather than on its Sophoclean consequences, the literary obligation—especially in a novel—is not fulfilled. Unlike Herman Melville or Thomas Mann, Steele evades the central problem of perversity by inventing a trick solution in shockingly new terms. The hocus-pocus switch from a deep moral problem to an antic social dilemma turns our initial terror and pity to grievous surprise and irritation. Potential tragedy dissipates in bizarre melodrama through, states one critic, "the instrumentality of no more august a *deus ex machina* than a moon-white cat."[14] Nevertheless, the Jamesian obliqueness is compelling. By stylistic felicities the author subtly attenuates into a short novel what is essentially a short story.

Delicately nuanced, the "literary" language is precise and highly restrained, yet fluid, and at times even preciously aphoristic: "Pizarro went away. And within a quarter of an hour he was back again to stand and stare into the blue. Space and escape. It was the blatantest of claptrap, of course, born of his need; the purest of 'dope' to allay the itch of his nerves and nip off and turn back underground the growth of his inscrutable consternation. As if a dog may escape by galloping any number of miles through space the can that's tied to its tail . . ." (70–71).

This attenuation suits his blurry Adam and Eve, who in the beginning, says Lloyd Morris, are "swayed by intimate and abstruse motives which they comprehend but imperfectly."[15] Louis Bromfield, while feeling the odd unreality of the tale, also noted "long stretches of undeniably powerful writing."[16] No other reviewer, however, went so far as Van Vechten Hostetter, who hailed *Taboo* as a novel of the "first water," ringing with "integrity and validity"—in short, "a shining golden needle in the haystack of contemporary fiction."[17] Disappointed by the "pretty small" sale of *Taboo* (only a few copies of Hemingway's *In Our Time* sold that year, but many thousands of Dreiser's *American Tragedy*), Steele felt that extreme reviews were better than "not much of either."[18]

Looking forward to another collection of his stories, Steele remained in Nantucket a few months before joining his family in Switzerland. As usual, the year's end held some surprises. The University of Denver dedicated its 1925 *Kynewisbok* to Steele. His superb "When Hell Froze" won first prize in the Harper Short Story Contest; *Best Stories* reprinted "Six Dollars"; and Steele's magnificent "The Man Who Saw Through Heaven" tied the O. Henry First Place Memorial Award—but Steele's previous prizes made him ineligible for the prize money.[19] As if Steele had not broken enough precedents, however, the committee also reprinted his "Blue Murder."

But Switzerland disappointed Steele, who looked upon it as "the deadest and most deadening land on earth."[20] During this 1925–26 winter, he hated words and loathed the idea of writing stories. Although he maintained that he never took himself or his work seriously, Steele now fretted. During the previous summer America's master story technician impressed the *Bookman* interviewer as a "very literary person indeed," for he "would say nothing whatever" about his reputation or the state of literature.[21] But during his Swiss depression, Steele confided to his family in

Denver that *Pictorial Review* was aiming for the "moron market."[22] The melancholiac recovered a little in February, however, when Harcourt, Brace published his third story collection.

CHAPTER 4

Urkey Island

*U*RKEY *Island* (1926) contains eight loosely connected stories arranged according to the chronology of their original appearance in *Pictorial Review* (1917–25): "White Hands," "Ching, Ching, Chinaman," "Wages of Sin," "Out of Exile," "Crocuses," " 'Lost at Sea,' " "Six Dollars," and "Out of the Wind." As in *Land's End*, salt air pervades *Urkey Island*. The stories melodramatize wild human eruptions in Steele's mythical fishing village off the New England coast. Isolated and generally somber, Urkey Island is a combination of Provincetown, Nantucket, and fancy. The Urkey stories purport to exist as highly conscious reconstructions of narrator Peter Means. Like Joe Manta of *Storm* and Jim Burden of Willa Cather's *My Antonia*, Peter sees himself retrospectively as a romantic sensibility. This point of view allows Steele great selectivity. Out of adolescent purblindness and false hearsay, seeing, and deduction, Peter re-creates his own elaborate confusions for the reader. Action moves from murkiness to clarity, but the reader never clearly sees the semiparticipating narrator himself.

Most reviewers liked *Urkey Island*'s mesmeric projections. One angry critic, however, labeled Steele's spasmodic prose "dismally aloof."[1] Beyond question were Steele's inventive power and esoteric rendering of the commonplace, but some perceptive readers felt that his illusory hold on the *lived* life was flaccid—that the *real* seemed to elude his technical brilliance. Sometimes his characters—rich, poor, pious, or sinful—act in ways contrary to what we know of human nature. Too often Steele's ministers, constables, drunks, and flirts are the puppets of melodramatic coincidence. More than in any other Steele collection, violent improbabilities dress in the garb of geometric inevitability. Allan Nevins lamented Steele's arbitrary events, but he also found *Urkey Island* a welcome change from Sarah Orne Jewett's "spinsterly fictions."[2]

Indeed, earlier New England local-colorists did not parade tabloid adultery, blackmail, theft, revenge, and murder. Like Edgar Lee Masters' *Spoon River Anthology, Urkey Island* depicts small-town tragedies in the revolt-from-the-village tradition. In fact, the New York *Times* viewed only Anderson's *Winesburg, Ohio* (and possibly *Land's End*) as superior to *Urkey Island.*

I *"White Hands"*

The mazy flummery of the first story, "White Hands," depends for its effect on the resolution of operatic insanity. With low-keyed intensity, Peter Means reconstructs the weird incidents in the hilltop house of wealthy Jed Pons, who laments his son's drowning. Old man Pons lingers at home with his veiled daughter-in-law, his brother Morris, and a housekeeper. "Can you imagine those four," asks the narrator, "gnawing at one another month by month, year after year, cooped together in that mysterious dwelling over our heads?" (6). In time, white-bearded Jed Pons ejects his grotesque brother, wills his fortune to his exotic daughter-in-law, and then dies. Because Jed Pons, an epileptic in the Poe tradition, had been almost buried alive once, he now lies in a custom-built vault with an *emergency* exit. Inevitably, the white-bearded ghost of Jed Pons is reported screeching clues to his daughter-in-law's guilt as he races over the moors.

This controlling incident permits Steele to unleash his portfolio of eerie atmospheric legerdemain. In the long-awaited end, the howling Urkey mob finds a broken-necked body in a stonepit—Jed's brother Morris wearing a white horsehair beard. Steele's clumsy vehicle for fathoming Morris' revengeful hocus-pocus is Peter Means' cousin, Constable Duncan: Morris was ousted from the hilltop house by Jed Pons for having made salacious advances toward his daughter-in-law, kept veiled from Urkey orthodoxy because she was a child bride. After the constable fits everything into place, nothing in the story seems to matter very much—only the picture of that white-bearded "ghost" screeching over the moors like a soul out of Dante's *Inferno.*

II *"Ching, Ching, Chinaman"*

Like "The Yellow Cat" of *Land's End*, "Ching, Ching, China-man" obfuscates. Here, however, Steele's foxy Oriental is the hero who dispels mystery rather than the peripheral shadow who sustains it. And the young narrator, Peter Means, learns in the end to qualify the sidewalk rhyme, "Ching, Ching, Chinaman ain't no good." In the story, which has a Chinese-puzzle plot, a former suitor, Snow, schemes to blast the marriage of well-off Sympathy Gibbs to the visionary Reverend Malden, a frustrated missionary. To blackmail letters requesting large sums of money and the separation of man and wife, Snow forges the signature of Sympathy's first husband, who had actually been lost at sea. Regarding themselves as adulterers with a bastard child, the two secretly comply. But the "unredeemed" Yen Sin discerns Snow's sinister hold over Malden. On his deathbed, the still unconverted Chinaman awes the villagers with his exposure of Snow, a druggist, who forthwith poisons himself.

Like many of the Urkey stories for *Pictorial Review,* this one is a foray into sheer escapism. Snow is incredibly vicious, Malden suspiciously obtuse, and Yen Sin fantastically acute. Although the plot is close to situation comedy, in theme and latitude the story suggests *The Scarlet Letter;* for brooding over Christless Yen Sin— one of the lost yellow millions—the frustrated Malden cries: "Confession! A sin confessed is no longer a sin" (50). The Snow-Malden relationship approximates the Chillingworth-Dimmesdale connection, and Sympathy Gibbs and daughter Hope are analogous to Hester Prynne and little Pearl. With its uneasy mixture of surface reality, spies on spies, philosophical sentimentalities on the Kiplingesque East-West theme, and Charlie Chan ratiocination, the story is indeed a literary hybrid short on art *and* nature.

Of limited appeal is the elaboration of such dialogue as: "Mista Yen Sin gottee name, allee light" (47). Steele's description of dancing Delia Manigault in "Conjuh" seems a fair way to describe this and most of his other *Pictorial Review* stories: "In despair she flung into another figure, more sophisticated and more intricate. This was what they wanted; the other was too naive and looked too easy. Calling on all her store of virtuosity, she added complication to complication."[3] The ending of "Ching, Ching Chinaman"—rain beats down on minister Malden as he prays for the soul of the heathen floating out to sea in his old laundry scow—is pure *kitsch.* Nevertheless, B. P. Schulberg of Preferred Pictures Studios hailed his film version—*Shadows,* starring Lon Chaney—as an advance of motion-picture art.

III   "The Wages of Sin"

In "The Wages of Sin" Peter Means witnesses a wife stealing money from her own husband in a café. Later, Peter learns that

the woman waiting out the storm and her husband's illness at a
local boardinghouse is from New York and is old Si Pilot's
daughter, Clara, who fifteen years before "got in trouble" and left
Urkey Island in disgrace. The villagers regard her marriage to the
older man as impurely motivated: "No wonder she had been taken
bad that evening, when she saw the lights of Urkey Village
coming out to engulf her and her dying, spending husband. For
a doomed rich man—who doesn't know—always has been and
always will be the hope of the Clara Pilots" (87).

Led by intoxicated Miah White (Clara's former beau), a mob
descends on the boardinghouse. Each villager is convinced that
providence has summoned Clara back to Urkey, before her childhood witnesses and judges; for, if the husband dies deluded,
leaving his fortune to Clara Pilot, the wages of sin lie on *them*.
After the rigmarole of communal search, the choruslike villagers
locate the pair in Si Pilot's old wagon. Weeping, Clara explains
that out of three hundred thousand dollars spent, six dollars remain in the dead man's pocket. She confesses that she stole her
husband's money and then returned it to permit him the illusion
of spending hugely until the very end. If she had never really
loved the man, she was at least grateful to him. As in other Urkey
stories, the narrator deludes the reader with appearance just as the
narrator himself was deluded.

IV   *"Out of Exile"*

Lewis Chrisman in the *Literary Digest* regarded "Out of Exile"
as a "powerful, rather disagreeable story, daring to the point of
being gruesome."[4] Peter Means recounts, through the dark glass
of his adolescence, the ironic melodrama of lovely Mary Matheson
and the Blake brothers. As a boy of six, Peter had once witnessed
the brothers' fight over Mary, in which the older brother Joshua
had threatened his gold-toothed younger brother Andrew with an
old dueling pistol. Incurably romantic, Mary declares that she
will marry the first brother who brings her a ring from the jeweler
across the sound. Andrew sets out in a storm, but Joshua vows to
stop him. After the storm, Joshua returns with the ring, and Mary
vows to marry him—but only after Andrew returns to stand at the
wedding.

During the next ten years, Peter Means himself falls in love
with Mary (twice his age), alterations in local color are set forth,
and Urkey gossip contends that Mary sent poor Andrew to his

death and has condemned poor Joshua to a life of single unbles-
sedness. One day, while standing at the gravestone for lost
Andrew, Joshua calls Mary a fool for waiting and confesses that
he actually saw Andrew drown but was unable to reach him.
When the wedding day is announced, the dull village becomes
idiotically emotional; but Peter is delighted when a gathering
storm and a shipwreck interrupt the wedding ceremony. Later
Mary convinces Joshua that the wedding can take place, for in
her hand she holds Andrew's gold-toothed skull, washed ashore in
a casketlike box. That night Peter's constable cousin reveals to
him a small round hole in the back of the skull and an old
dueling-pistol bullet lodged neatly within.

V *"Crocuses"*

Plot in "Crocuses" is as melodramatically intricate as in "Ching,
Ching, Chinaman," but the round and subtle main character,
Buchanan Gowd, also commands attention. Once a power in the
land, the great lawyer, after clearing local citizens of charges
such as murder or theft, habitually retreated to his brick-walled
solitude to tend crocuses which bloomed each spring to spell
BESS, the name of his dead wife: "It's odd, you'll say, to have
found that sort of sentimental weakness in an iron and granite
man. I think it was not odd at all. In every house there must be
a door, and in every character some breach for the spirit to come
and go" (138). The perfect creature of an age when failure was
shameful, Gowd was hard, alert, ruthless, rich, and friendless; but
the grown narrator now sees the legendary lawyer as a broken
man, shaggy and gray.

An incident unfolds: out of professional pride, the lawyer had
earlier accepted philandering Amos Dyer's divorce suit against
his young wife, an Urkey saint; too late, Jenny Dyer herself comes
to Gowd for defense. Believing her innocent, the lawyer tears up
his retainer; but in court—in a time of illiberal divorce laws—he
shames her ruthlessly. Afterward, in the flood time of his powers,
Gowd quits his practice: "I've made enough money. Time to give
the young ones a chance" (144). A month later, the old warrior
sits in Miah White's weir shed: "There Gowd sat by the hour, by
the day, by the week, it seemed, arguing his final case for a defense, putting his immortal soul in cross-examination before the
bar of his immortal soul" (146). Gowd's problem: should a
lawyer turn a "guilty" man away? One day, when his house burns

down, the fire destroys all his legal papers—"ghosts" of men good
and bad. Moving to a hillside shack, the village eccentric digs a
garden, walling it against the slanting knoll like a picture frame,
his "microscopic assiduity" a labor "epic and enormous" (151).

When Gowd dies, he leaves behind a month-old will—sardonic,
mocking, and "locked and bolted and double-guaranteed to stand"
(158): to wit, if no one enters the exposed garden for six months,
seven of Gowd's former clients get equal shares of his fortune;
if *any* person enters the enclosure, the money goes to Jenny Dyer.
Inevitably folks talk, but it is a gossiping seed man who plants
the idea in many heads that, before Gowd had died, he had
bought enough crocus bulbs to write the names of all the sinners
he had whitewashed in court. When the Hyannis Bar Association
moves to establish a decent monument for Gowd in the Urkey
graveyard, the pricked communal conscience joins in—but guard-
ing the hillside is executor Miah White, "clinging insanely to the
crazy letter of the daft testament" (176).

On the horns of a dilemma, the seven guilty clients desire the
legacy but not the attendant exposure. As in Mark Twain's "Man
That Corrupted Hadleyburg," a fascinating but altogether fantastic communal meeting provides the embattled context for the
complicated document. Some citizens favor decent burial for
Gowd and support for the unknown sinners; others hold out for
the status quo and exposure. To heighten the fanaticism, exiled
Jenny Dyer enters the fray. Unable to resist, the heirs charge the
garden fence; but, before they can dig up the crocuses, they are
arrested for trespassing. A week later the spring flowers bloom
into beautiful patterns. Only Buchanan Gowd's self-chosen words
on his small granite slab are evident: *"Blind, he kept the faith of
the blind."*

VI " *'Lost at Sea'* "

In several Urkey stories Peter Means alludes to "LOST AT
SEA"— a piece of statuary among the tilted gravestones of Rigg's
Dome. In the story Peter's visiting friend Patgon, a mainland
sculptor, crusades to ship the monument to a museum, but he
later affirms its rightful place on Rigg's Dome. Patgon's presence,
however, refurbishes the legend of "LOST AT SEA" about the
inseparable trio of wryneck Andrew Sparks, mighty Israel Atwood, and the beautiful Phila who had lived out their schoolday
adventures in "mild-wild" Urkey. Before long, Phila blooms to

ladyhood; Israel chases the whale; and Andy retreats to his debt-ridden stone yard where he cherishes his memories. His shock at the wedding of Israel and Phila dramatizes his physical and psychological isolation.

But, not long afterward, Andy is the first to hear from Phila that Israel is lost at sea. Together they decide on a great white block of Rutland statuary as a memorial. Andy chisels into the monolith the words "LOST AT SEA"; and he insists that Phila pay him only *after* the statue is finished. The narrator convincingly chronicles Andy's birth as an artist. After his handyman chores he would rush up the hillside: "And there, safe at last in the solitude of the sky and the dead, he would kneel down before the raw white shaft to unbuckle his kit, his fingers bungling everything in their eagerness to be at work" (212). Envisioning godlike Israel imprisoned in the cold hard rock, Andy after several weeks shears off two corners, and the townsfolk consider the marble ruined and Andy mad. Indeed, points out Patgon, Andy as artist was slightly mad or sublimely ignorant or both. Haunting the scene of Andy's creative demolition, Phila, too, sees Israel in the stone; but the townspeople still see a "biled onion" with rough features—but not Israel's.

As in so many Steele stories, the lost often return; Israel is no exception. Refusing to believe that her husband is back, Phila runs away, but Andy retrieves her. A week later she recovers matrimonial paradise; but Andy is now lost, perhaps a suicide at sea. In his studio a year later, the sculptor Patgon reveals to Peter Means an old daguerreotype of Andrew Sparks. Patgon explains: Andrew Sparks moved inevitably into that unconscious realm where admiration for friend and loathing for self fused in "LOST AT SEA"—a stony portrait of the wryneck artist as a young whaling captain, drowned off the Horn. Steele's cunning dramatization of the power of the artist's imagination to reconcile opposites is Coleridgean; but, by explaining all things through a "transcendental figure," Patgon here and Duncan elsewhere, Steele simultaneously surprises *and* insults our intellect.

VII   "*Six Dollars*"

In "Six Dollars" the narrator reveals the tormented life of Urkey Village banker Tansy Snow. As a youthful clerk, Tansy—guided by a small garret lamp—several times rows to Stone Fold islet. Under a moonlit thorn tree he makes love to Donna Salisbury, old Shepherd Cabe's dull, motherless daughter. But sensing the need for respectability in his new position, Tansy sheepishly ends the rustic affair by handing the simple girl his week's wages—six dollars. Back in Urkey Village, he concludes uneasily that "you can't pay God with money"; and, after secretly repenting, he suddenly feels himself "whiter than snow" and capable of becoming the "biggest man in town."

When the reformed Tansy becomes assistant cashier of the bank, he marries Elsie Baker, his ideal of earthly love and of religious reverence. But Tansy nightly peers restlessly through their bedroom window at brightly lighted Stone Fold. Unlike his ambitious, civic-minded wife, unsociable Tansy more and more sits alone upstairs in the dark bedroom and studies the constant light. Like Hawthorne's Dimmesdale, he broods on secret sin; the light ray poisons his thoughts. Angry, alarmed, fascinated, he rows on foggy nights toward the islet to discern the light. Finally he senses that in this faithful shepherdess is not spite, only the high tragedy of unrequited love. Tansy's inverted view of Stone Fold is Theocritan—the conventional view of a relatively complex and urbanized man looking back nostalgically to his pastoral golden age of simple and idyllic love:

Little by little as he watched the fallen star, or thought of it shining in secret there, he forgot to hear the busy voices below; he heard the wind running in gray grasses and the living sound of breakers on far-strewn reefs and the dry rustle of leaves in the thorn-tree. And what had happened was that he was no longer surrounded by walls and gables and hemmed in by the thoughts and needs and elbows of hundreds of industrious little two-legged vegetables; the walls had melted, his horizon was the horizon of dark ocean, and he walked in space. (244)

In imaginary dialogues, childless Tansy and his elemental earth-goddess Donna murmur love matches on eros, fertility, and birth. For ten years, Tansy Snow nurses his sin in private. Finally, to prevent a billboard from blotting the beautiful Urkey landscape (actually to prevent it from blocking the bedroom view), reticent Tansy spellbinds the village council. Elsie envisions him in Congress; but, when party members call at his home, Tansy is on darkened Stone Fold with ancient Grandfather Cabe. A horde of illegitimate children occupies the old house. Tansy gazes upon Donna Salisbury lying in state in the parlor flooded with light from a polished lamp still bearing the revengeful price tag—$6.00. "Some folks," concludes the narrator, "have a God of mercy. And some have a terrible God" (260).

VIII   *"Out of the Wind"*

"Out of the Wind" is a circular story on the themes of time and the love that binds. The Coffin sisters, born a year apart, grow up in a sturdy middle-class brick house. For seventeen years they live in love and mutual sympathy, sleeping in the same bed and confiding secrets. Although Ray, the younger sister, will sacrifice her love for wild fisherman Eddie Franklin to Molly, the older sister, chance plays the younger sister into the fisherman's net— and the older sister marries frugal storekeeper George Dunker. Enemies since boyhood, the brothers-in-law transfer all their ill-will to their wives who sympathize with each other silently, but they remain loyal to their husbands who quarrel over the disposition of the sisters' family house.

Although "Out of the Wind" has no atmospheric oppressiveness, the physical contrast between the sisters' living conditions is clearly realized: the older sister's brick-and-slate Victorian mansion and the younger's jerry-built marsh cottage; Molly's starched society and Ray's kitchen beer drinkers; Molly's two children and Ray's brood. For eighteen years the sisters live their separate lives, each in her own way, until each charges the other with recriminations: Molly's first son and Ray's first daughter fall into a Romeo-and-Juliet-type love affair in high school, elope, and are heard of no more. During the next twelve years, each sister oscillates between pride in and contempt for her husband, and the narrator peppers his story of generations with reflective commentary.

The climax occurs when old drunken Ed Franklin loses his boat and house to creditor George Dunker, picks up a mallet, and frightens his brother-in-law to death. Fleeing the scene of his crime, the fisherman falls through a trap door and breaks his neck. Neither touches the other man; yet both are dead. After attending with loyal pain their husbands' funerals, the widows meet in the sturdy old family manse. In bed together, warmed by a fireplace and secure against the wind, the two old sisters (like characters out of Sarah Orne Jewett's *Deephaven*) plan a flower garden.

O'Brien selected "Out of the Wind" for his *Best Stories of 1926;* and the O. Henry Committee, unable to deny Steele the legitimate fruits of his victories, presented him with the first award for "Bubbles," a story Steele had written during his dismal winter the year before in Switzerland. (Sherwood Anderson received the second award for "Death in the Woods.") Under a new dispensation, Harper arranged with Steele for a new novel—one to be serialized in *Harper's Magazine* before book publication. Detaching himself as much as possible from such literary neighbors and conversationalists as Howard Brubaker, William McFee, and Henrik Van Loon, Steele began work on his novel in Westport. The following summer in Nantucket, he continued to labor on the novel between rounds of story writing. His fourth story collection—far superior to *Urkey Island*—was published in the fall.

CHAPTER *5*

The Man Who Saw Through Heaven

*T*HE *Man Who Saw Through Heaven and Other Stories* (1927)
contains twelve selections, seven originally published in *Harper's Magazine* (1919–27) and five in *Pictorial Review* (1924-27).
All but three of the weaker stories—"The Thinker," "What Do You
Mean—Americans?" and "Luck"—Steele first published in magazines during his strong 1925–27 years. Along with these three
stories and his classic title story, the fourth collection includes
"Sooth," "Sailor! Sailor!," "Bubbles," "Blue Murder," "When Hell
Froze," "Autumn Bloom," "A Drink of Water," and "Fe-Fi-Fo-
Fum." Unlike the Urkey stories, these display a greater variety
of themes and techniques.

Reviewers praised the collection, often without qualification;
but some still insisted that Steele's indirection and Euclidian
plots prevented him from getting closer to life—and, therefore,
from becoming as great a writer as he was an artist. Although
these stories unfold as much as ever through implication and
suggestion, they show—compared to the wild Urkey tales—
greater restraint, cautious use of coincidence, and sharper motivation. In the best stories, the characters, whatever their extraordinary postures, seem more human. Few stories, for example,
rely for effect on the over-used Urkey device of labyrinthine
revenge or retribution; instead, more stories treat the protagonist's
awakening, be he youth or adult, well or sick.

The New York *Times* reviewer, observing Steele's tricky irony
of circumstance (close to that of O. Henry, Sophocles, or Hardy),
wondered how any committee naming itself after O. Henry could
award prizes so consistently to stories "so cruel in essence."[1] But
Clifton Fadiman, writing for the *Nation*, was amazed by Steele's
"really marvelous ingenuity"—how he could break the "laws" of
the conventional popular story and yet avail himself of them:
"The basis of Mr. Steele's art is melodrama—but melodrama so
subtly stylized and refined, so outwardly conventional, as to be

hardly recognizable."[2] Less a champion of stories cruel in essence rather than of, say, Katherine Mansfield's terrifying closeness, Fadiman and other young reviewers and critics, extolling Ernest Hemingway's "The Killers," encouraged the liberation of the American short story from sentimentality—to which Steele would subscribe; but he would not help free it from ironic melodrama and neat plot. With relief, champions of the iconoclastic Anderson and Hemingway might well turn even to Zona Gale's "simple, jagged little life-stories" and away from Steele's "fervent complexities."[3]

I *"The Man Who Saw Through Heaven"*

In the tight compass of "The Man Who Saw Through Heaven" —one of the world's great stories—Steele powerfully dramatizes the history of mankind's spiritual evolution. The story, structured as search and pursuit, is an evolutionary compendium, a Darwinian nutshell, wherein ontogeny assumes phylogeny. Of all his stories, this one—its roots in Steele's youthful study of astronomy at the University Park Observatory—most satisfied the usually dissatisfied author: "No one knew what I was writing about—an ironic story of a man, a missionary, creating God in his own image. I suppose it was a rebellion against my ministerial background. And what happened? My father loved it. Religious magazines still ask to use it. I explain. They still want it."[4]

In brief, a complacent Fundamentalist missionary, his Christian orthodoxies shattered by the impact of scientific naturalism, plummets within. Fearful, the Reverend Hubert Diana forsakes wife and duty to plunge into African darkness. In village after village he harangues the natives, leaving in his monomaniacal wake mud images of his everchanging god: first, star-swallowing blobs; then reptiles; then beasts; and, finally, just before he dies in peace, a figure of God in the image of man. This movement from Conradian "darkness" to Steelean "light" covers perhaps five hundred thousand years in the life of man but only four in the life of Steele's allegorical hero.

Steele brilliantly foreshortens time and controls the presentation of events by using an anonymous but reliable narrator. As in so many of Steele's tales which are scaled for both credibility and mystery, the first section of "The Man Who Saw Through Heaven" does not really begin the action but establishes the narrator's attitude toward his material, sets up numerous foreshadow-ings and anticipations, and justifies his joining orthodox Mrs. Cora Diana's bizarre African safari in search of her husband. The narrator's employment as an insurance agent and Mrs. Diana's perseverance might be sufficient justification, but the significant moral link to the narrator's involvement in the historic expedition—exterior and interior—is his troubled conscience; for he personally, as a diversion, had conducted the clergyman to the Boston Observatory before the missionary party sailed: "Had it not been for that kindly intentional 'hunch' of mine, the astounded eye of the Reverend Hubert Diana would never have gazed through the floor of Heaven, and he would never have undertaken to measure the Infinite with the foot rule of his mind" (2).

Because the report of Diana's adventures is reconstructed out of the narrator's progressive involvement—out of what he knows and hears—details which might impede the forward and upward thrust of the heavily implicated adventure are credibly eliminated. Though Steele relied on this technique of selectivity in stories earlier than *Urkey Island,* he had never managed it so perfectly. Then, too, the semibewildered insurance agent gains the reader's trust by being closer intellectually to a Jamesian central intelligence. The narrator insists on Diana's fanaticism—the missionary's extravagant behavior that results from his gaining only a literal glimpse of the figurative truth. The awesome telescopic view—not simply grist for Diana's sermon mill—so dislocates his values that, like naked Adam, he finds himself alienated from innocence. He imagines that our universe is merely one in a cluster of universes and that this cluster is a new atomic category of universes—as small as the stone in his opal ring. And perhaps the hypothetical ring is worn on the tentacle of some vast organism, or, as the amused Boston astronomer puts it, "some inchoate creature hobnobbing with its cloudy kind in another system of universes—which in turn—" (9). Ironic as is Diana's odyssey or pilgrim's progress, he at least escapes the intolerable burden of solipsism and comes full circle to a magnified "human" God with whom he can talk via cataclysm and conviction rather than by a personally untested inherited faith.

In the climactic end, however, shallow Mrs. Diana, powerful in her thin-lipped meekness and serene faith, understands neither her "idolatrous" husband nor his entrance (illusory or real) into the heart of lightness at the village of Little Tara—an atmospheric synthesis of light and dark, of America and Africa, of civilization without skepticism, and of faith without barbarism. So great is the pressure of the evolutionary "content" on the short-story "form" that "The Man Who Saw Through Heaven" verges on bursting its bounds. Most writers, no doubt, would have found the Reverend Diana's adventure more suitable for a big novel, a trilogy, or even an entire canon.

II   *"Sooth"*

Combining the inner freedom of the incoherent literary experimenters with the technical correctness of the rigid literary conservatives, "Sooth" deals with the wanton destruction which the "higher" creatures universally bestow on the "lower" ones. Thinking a shark plies the night waters, a Negro rum-runner, Roboam, casually harpoons a seal; in turn, a thrill-seeking white flapper, Tilly, unknowingly shoots the crewman while hunting seals. That Tilly kills Roboam comes as no surprise; for the girl craves greater "kicks," and the Negro is fearfully convinced that a dancing white girl with "di'monds in huh ears" will murder him.

In this melodrama Steele relies on anticipation for the dreaded effect of folly and waste. The omniscient viewpoint presents both "lives"—first the white girl's, then the black man's. Tilly, racing over moonlit moors in an older man's sleek car, resembles the "jazzy" rebels in Fitzgerald's tales about flaming youth. A twenty-year-old child, she carmines her lips from a little gold vanity case and looks upon everything—companion, dancing, drinking, duck-and-rabbit shooting—as deadly pallid. Life, she feels, owes her a few more thrills—painful ones. Not seeking thrills, but remembering his life as a series of adventurous aliases, Roboam religiously knows that long ago back in Georgia what the soothsayer had said was "sooth."

Now, wantonly swimming after two cow seals after harpooning their mate, Roboam finds himself cavorting with them instead; and then, like a Rousseauistic child, he romantically senses a bond: "More keenly he wished that it were not merely a strange and beatific interlude; that he were indeed a seal, the same big-shouldered bull he had slain; and that he might go on forever with these twins, striking out boldly on long migrations across the empty seas, diving through green caverns where no man was known, rolling and rollicking in the slant sunlight of lost beaches, riding the tops of storm-billows and laughing at the storm" (59). By juxtaposing fragments of the old soothsayer's prophecy, Tilly's gleeful comments on her own marksmanship, and Roboam's bewildered last utterances, Marxist critics would embrace the occult story as a politico-racial allegory of reckless consumer and apprehensive consumed.

III   *"Sailor! Sailor!"*

The arid plain south of young Danny Steele's Denver is the ironic scene of the Arcadian memoir "Sailor! Sailor!" Reminiscing about the humdrum Rockies as compared to the adventurous High Line Ditch, the narrator recalls how, as a romantic inland boy, he had transformed the stream into an ocean. In its use of the micro-macrocosm, "Sailor! Sailor!" resembles Jonathan Swift's *Gulliver's Travels* and Mark Twain's *The Mysterious Stranger*:

Lying on one's stomach with the chin nearly in the water, the fifteen-foot spread of slowly sweeping, coffee-colored water widened in the swift perspective of the plains-boy's dream. Ripples grew waves, waves blue rollers creamed with spume, or black waves where storms wandered and ships drove aslant with singing spars, or green glass again where privateersmen warped through the windless stealth of tropic moonlights, or the Swiss Family plundered their wreck, or Easy rowed ashore. And once, on a day never to be forgotten, with my living eyes there, low to the water, I saw a living fish. (68)

Nostalgically, the author recalls a great adventure. Grazing the South Side herd, Dan and his friends seize upon rancher Flack's unexpected invitation to raid his surplus melons. Inside the barbwire, however, they have to flee from the new owner and his pregnant wife. Later one hot summer day the new rancher comments with nautical enthusiasm about Dan's little ship in the High-Line Ditch. The boy is further amazed when the rancher, turning his tools to a pine block and assorted scraps, fashions a remarkable vessel. The rancher—resembling "Gulliver in the frontispiece" (77)—launches the ship from the opposite shore; and Dan quickly fashions a dock. Then the man restations the custom, sets right the chandlery, zigzags the "Rio" streets, and weaves his Cornish monologue through the Colorado gusts, the city of inches, and the youth's romantic imagination: through

juxtaposition and climactic arrangement, the boy sees an expressionistic montage of wooden legs, hooked hands, tatooed
arms, a bar maid calling *Marino! Marino!* to her lover, drunkenness, brawling, and finally, escape—flight by sea to a dry land a
thousand miles away. In the tumult of therapeutic play, however,
the tiny boat capsizes and the seaman-rancher trudges to his
gatemaking.

Impressively disenchanted by the exemplum, the boy returns
to the herd and grimly responds to his waiting companions: "He
says we should keep out o' his melons, or we'll see" (87). Thus
Steele dramatizes how reality shocks romantics young and old,
how rude awakenings shatter escapist dreams—how human voices
wake us and we drown.

IV "Bubbles"

Like little Maisie Farange in James' *What Maisie Knew*, "go-
ing-on-seven" Carol Bonaparte in "Bubbles" leads a wandering
life, garnished with the cruelty of parental sexual intrigue—one
reason, no doubt, for the story's early popularity. Both Maisie
and Carol rely for consistent affection on their governesses; and
for a coherent reality, both strain to piece together a bizarre
jigsaw puzzle world. And, though the intricacies of the two narratives unfold by way of unreliable mentalities, both writers
tactfully convey a larger context. Steele represents the quality
of Carol's mind through simple words, ideas, and syntax: "It
was late at night and it was a strange house, a strange room and
a strange bed. Strangest of all was the getting to bed" (101).

More than she knows things, the semiprecocious Carol feels
them. She feels, for example, that something is wrong when
Daddy—wealthy and cosmopolitan—briefly hires a "governess,"
a "nurse," or a "secretary" but continues to let middle-aged Miss
Eliza Codd (Coddie) do all the governing, nursing, and secre-
tarial work. Residing in hotels in America and in Europe, Carol
often feels a sharp politeness between Daddy and Coddie. Proud,
but at the same time jealous of her "man-about-town" father,
Carol prefers him just *after* the departure of one of the ladies—
the one who wept, the one who adored perfume, the one who
smoked black cigarettes—not when he grows fidgety again and
sports evening clothes and cigarettes instead of tweeds and pipes.

That Carol's mother is ill, not dead, suggests itself during a
"tweedy" period at a resort when a letter with a "funny" address—

Dr. Kamp's House—arrives. Dreamlike tags of dispute between Daddy and Coddie precede Carol's numbness at the train depot when, without Coddie, she and Daddy journey to The Pasture, the Connecticut River mansion of Carol's birth. Promised a "regular" governess and a "surprise," Carol falls asleep in the strange house, her bedfellow a kitten named Bubbles. At first, the readers assume that "Mrs. Lephant" is Carol's mother, a red-wristed, grizzle-haired woman who drops Bubbles to prove that cats always land right-side up. Hiding from the hated woman, Carol spies another, pale and oddly familiar: "by her slender, prettily clad figure and her silk stockings and high-heeled shoes, Carol knew her of a sudden for what she was. She was the new governess" (108).

But this Mary Poppins is really her mother, Stacia Bonaparte. Helplessly talkative, Daddy makes a gallant effort to welcome home his convalescent wife, a woman of extraordinary quietude. Although the child wishes to hold her mother, Stacia simply suggests that Carol be *her* kitten. Terror later strikes the child when the somnolent Stacia clutches her hand under the dining table. The next morning Carol finds Bubbles in the tall grass, her neck broken: "Somewhere aloft some one was laughing. It was low but unmuffled and pure, wandering, softly jubilating, soliloquizing, a little sarabande of mirth" (123). After a confusion of un-Poesque trunks and telegrams, bewildered Carol is relieved to learn from crestfallen and thoroughly modern Daddy that, yes, Stacia was just another "governess"—and Coddie joins them on the train.

The title "Bubbles" suggests that Stacia Bonaparte is as irresponsible as a kitten: "Impetuously loved, profoundly depended upon, she [Bubbles] seemed to take perverse delight in maintaining her own poise and doing as she sweetly pleased" (105–6). Also, the wishful bubbles of father and daughter seem doomed to burst. Finally, the true state of affairs between Daddy and Coddie—like a Browning poem—tantalizes through undemonstrable ironies.

V *"Luck"*

After the plethora of barbs tossed at Steele for his devotion to the improbable, it seemed inevitable that sooner or later he would dramatize the problem of chance, as he did in "Luck" (1919). Its setting of frigidity and remoteness, its activities of poker and cheating, emotions of hate and fear, and its theme of free will and determinism suggest an equally ironic but less pessimistic variation on Stephen Crane's "Blue Hotel." Good fortune surrounds one mountain man; steady reversal, the other.

Steele's robust, generous, beef-grower Will Yaard scoffs at the notion of luck; a man, he is convinced, directs his own fate and generates his own prosperity. After the folk drama of all-night poker in the rear of a mountain store, Yaard pauses on his long walk home to inform the cheating Jennison—spendthrift, drunk, loafer—that he is doomed to fail in God's world. Yaard reveals his own successful formula of moderation: "The whole thing is, I work hard, but not too hard. I use my head, but I don't worry. I'll take a drink, but I don't take too many. I'll do a fool thing maybe, once in a long while, like tonight; but here's the point— you won't find me doing it *twice*. And so I'll keep on going ahead. Bound to!" (142).

To prevent Yaard from marrying the Judge's daughter, the enraged Jennison plans to kill himself, hoping that Yaard will be charged with murdering him. Borrowing Yaard's old revolver, Jennison burns his winnings, shoots himself, tosses the revolver near a bush, and manages to drop dead in a hole in lake ice. The denouement then shifts the point of view backward in time and focuses on Yaard and the Judge—*who luckily happens by on his sled!* From the hilltop *both* men witness Jennison's erratic movements. Under warm sled robes, innocent of the twist of fate, accident, providence, or whatever, Yaard ignores the Judge's comment about how lucky he, Yaard, is to catch a ride home on such a cold morning. Because Steele fused the *idea of fate* with character and action, his use of Aristotle's cautionary improbable possible is less objectionable in this story than in some others.

VI   *"Blue Murder"*

In 1930 editor Blanche Williams extolled the shrouded inevitability of "Blue Murder": "For motive, for stupidity aptly enough ascribed, and for justice measured without patent contriving, the story has no equal in one of its length among all tales of crime."[6] Steele, however, felt that it was the "worst story I have ever had the misfortune to write."[6] Like Hawthorne, Steele often uses the mystifying or skeptical device of alternative possibility; but, since "Blue Murder" achieves its effect through "fair" or "unfair" deception, only the second "perfect reading" exhibits a detective-story simultaneity of concealment and disclosure. Then the truth becomes as obvious, the outcome as inevitable, as the anecdote of Columbus and the egg.

Besides the name of the disreputable Wyoming stallion, the title itself suggests nocturnal felony. The surface or first-reading story presents farmer Jim Bluedge returning from the railroad station with a blurry silhouette—the wild stallion in tow. Shortly after Jim's grand arrival, the chorus of neighbors finds him dead, his head and chest caved in, the fence broken, and the stallion racing up the mountainside: "No outlash here of heels in fright. Here was a forefoot. An attack aimed and frontal; an onslaught reared, erect; beast turned biped; red eyes mad to white eyes aghast . . ." (171). Nursing a sore neck, Jim's dull brother Cam picks up a length of chain and his blacksmith hammer and rushes up the mountainside after the crazy horse. Another brother, Frank, consoles the dead man's wife; the next day Frank himself is found up the mountainside, his backbone crushed by a fore shoe. Vowing sole revenge on the stallion, the returning Cam that night unchains Blue Murder from a hiding place, rides him to the smithy, and heats a horseshoe white hot.

An intense four-link chain of determinism or poetic justice occurs: Cam trips over a nail box, causing him to scorch the stallion, so that the tormented horse kicks, and the broken-necked Cam falls dead on the sizzling horseshoe. When neighbors find the third brother dead, they also discover an unshod—a never shod—Blue Murder. Thus the subsurface or second-reading story emerges: Out of stupid resentment, "unimaginative" Cam has murdered first one brother and then, in self-defense, the other. Numerous clues point to the character of the sullen, hammer-swinging Cam. An unshod Blue Murder is suggested when the neighbors hear the stallion's "soft thunder of hoofs" and when Cam himself (after hammering down the fence) sees to the right of the runaway horse "a faint shower of sparks . . . where herding mares wheeled" (170). Having killed Jim with a horseshoe from his leather blacksmith's apron, Cam is shocked when he realizes that the stallion pounding up the stony slope is unshod. Before the others can capture the horse, Cam sets out. Meanwhile, Frank inspects the soft paddock earth and realizes what has happened; but, greedy for Jim's property and lusting after Jim's wife, he, too, falls victim to Cam's crashing horseshoe.

As in "White Horse Winter," the sensation of a wild stallion on the loose excites the imagination, but the atmosphere of "Blue

Murder" is less wonderful than sinister. Gothic storm, smithy hell flames, satanic blacksmith—these melodramatically symbolize evil. And in this Vulcanic context, Jim's coquettish wife, Blossom, is a village Venus who bears the same name as the dormitory wanton in "How Beautiful with Shoes."

VII *"When Hell Froze"*

"When Hell Froze"—Steele's *Harper's* Prize Story about a farm wife whose kindness to a stranger results in cruel misunderstanding—continues to be popular.[7] For eighteen years lovely Addie Joslin has fortified her husband's land and stock. A "slow" woman, she feels at one with the soil, the animals, her husband, and her two sons. Waiting for her husband and eldest son to return from the annual business trip to New York, Addie is cordial to the vagabond who asks for work. As it turns out, he is on his way to town to work in the garage of Addie's brother-in-law. While waiting for the menfolk to drive home from the train, the wandering mechanic plays tunes on his harmonica—including "Kiss Me Again." Addie's little son Frankie, who misinterprets the man's throaty recital of the final phrase, asks his mother why she is kissing the stranger. (The stranger's song is a variation on the lighthouse inspector's use of blocks in "Ropes.") Amused by the boy's notion that his mother is buying tunes with kisses, the man gives Frankie the harmonica. Guessing that the menfolk will not return that day, Addie kindly takes a free snack to the wayfarer. His oblique but good-natured parting propositions slightly fluster her.

When the men do return late that night, Addie happily prepares supper. Her husband, Joslin, bestows one of his two yearly kisses; and her son Ray matter-of-factly explains that they forgot a pair of aprons for her on the train. When Ray later plays a few notes on Frankie's harmonica and asks where it came from, tired Addie simply replies: "Somebody or other give it to him, I guess" (206). To complicate matters, the sounds wake up Frankie who wants his harmonica—the one, he says, from the man his mother kissed. Finding illogicality wearisome, Addie simply denies it; and then, exasperated, she threatens to spank her child if ever he repeats his lie. Undressing for bed, Addie ponders routine chores and decisions, but underlying these she feels her identity with the soil . . . and wonders about the color of the lost aprons.

Avoiding her the next day, both Ray and Frankie sulk at supper.

When serge-suited Ray, angry and audacious, stalks out of the
house, Addie protects him by telling Joslin that she has sent the
boy to the store. And, when Frankie volunteers that he *never*
told Ray about the stranger, Addie is relieved to learn that Ray's
anger is based on a silly misunderstanding. When Ray returns,
however, she feels helpless and panicky and, as the days slip by,
unjustly punished. One afternoon, when Joslin returns from the
gossipy Crossing, he coldly asks about all the "talk." Taken
aback, Addie stammers ignorance. Raging, Joslin is now convinced of his wife's unfaithfulness. At supper Addie summons
up the simple explanation, but Frankie, frightened, cannot con-
firm it. Pushing the "dirty" food away, father and son stalk out.

Daily, the men eat unpalatable store food by the kitchen drain,
until face-saving Joslin prepares a can of lye water. When he
tells his wife to wash her hands in it, Addie replies: "You can
leave it there till hell freezes over" (222). Later in the fields
three out-of-towners with upturned collars accuse her of un-
Christian conduct; rushing home, Addie there finds the minister
who bids the family kneel and pray. Amid the supplications of
mooing cows, the prayers of the minister rise up until, renewed,
Joslin and son dip their own sinful hands in the lye water. Ada-
mant, Addie runs off into the night to town.

During the long winter, the all-male family deteriorates to the
point where Ray finally telephones Addie, now a hatseller in a
shop. Expecting his mother's return that night, the youth challenges his stubborn father about the can of lye water, replenished
each week with a cup of water. In the middle of their quarrel a
slimmer, prettier Addie walks in with her suitcases and explains
that Mr. Hedge (the mechanic) has been good to her this
winter but that hell froze over long ago. When Joslin simply replies, "Well, wife?," "She walked to the drain board and, laying
her gloves and the harmonica among the dishes, she dipped her
hands into the lye, then drew them out and held them away to
dribble on the floor. A spot of pink lay on either cheek bone and
her eyes were as shiny as dry diamonds" (236). All break into
soft laughter. Upstairs, Addie slips a new harmonica under
Frankie's pillow. She now realizes that the land, the stock, the
men—all are a part of her; but she, after all, is not a part of them.
Independent, self-possessed, she chooses to remain, simply out
of expediency or simply out of a woman's love.

VIII   *"Autumn Bloom"*

In "Autumn Bloom" another wife waits for her husband—this time from a business trip to Cleveland on the steamer. With this common motif, Steele ironically depicts the theological doctrine: "I believe in the resurrection of the body." But the story is marred by the fictional cliché of amnesia. News of the steamer's explosion and her husband's death comes to Cora Sailor by way of her husband's partner. With the partner and her son, Cora finds herself in a montage of taxis and corpses. Finally she identifies her husband by the flimsy evidence of coat and Elk ring. Confessing a premonition of her husband's death, Cora weeps in lonely grief. As no one else can, the widow now embraces the "whole" man. Cora flaunts her tears—not for her husband's death, but for his resurrection. Her brilliant autumn garden is a metaphor for her present life.

The overworked device of amnesia occurs when a newspaper-man informs the widow that he recognized her husband and helped revive him. Finally, the train (like a star out of the East) arrives with her husband aboard. Two O. Henry surprises follow: a voice informs Cora that outside Finboro her husband's heart simply stopped; and, before Cora's consciousness can hear her unconscious whisper, "Are they *sure?*," she herself dies.

IX   *"A Drink of Water"*

As one act of kindness changes Addie Joslin's life, so too does one of unkindness alter Clare Mayo's. Although Clare's state of mind and unusual circumstances in "A Drink of Water" justify her "cry-wolf" act of negation, her guilt pushes her into relinquishing an ideal of specialized love for her practice of general "service." Instead of dramatizing Clare's guilt, however, Steele tacitly juxtaposes the two Clares: after and before. The "after" Clare is a thirty-five-year-old blonde whose simplistic altruism puzzles gentlemen who prefer blondes. The "before" Clare—before her "fall"—is a narcissistic twenty-eight-year-old careerist who believes in preserving her love for that one man in the world for whom it is "meant."

Spending her two-week vacation away from repulsive woman-chasers, Clare rents a semi-isolated beach shack; the Atlantic Ocean is on one side, quicksand ponds on the other. Nearly drowned, she is saved at one point by a handsome young man;

but, savoring the thought of elemental violence and her long-awaited angel, she feigns unconsciousness until, hoping for a heartbeat, the young man touches her breast. She automatically recoils, whereupon the young man, laughing bitterly, walks away. Clare's awareness of literary irony offsets threadbare Romanticism: "There was a joke there if one wanted to look at it. The weeks of anticipation. The opening panic. The liberation. The undertow. Death. Resurrection. The hero. All those steps of a dramatic preparation, like a story in a book. And then—" (277).

In place of Clare's hero, a tweedy forty-year-old, shyly flirtatious, happens by. Abruptly Clare returns to her shack. With wistful excitement, the man pursues her, foolishly asking for a drink of water. Angrily complying, Clare then closes the door in his face. To save his dignity, the insulted man bangs on it. Footsteps at the farther door increase suspense, but they belong to the neighbor woman, with whom Clare holds forth on life and love. Although Clare agrees with "Mrs. Eccles" (a kept woman) that many men need not an ocean but only a cup of love, the young girl is incensed to hear that she, like the older woman, is born to "serve" men and cannot change her "type." Later, unable to fall asleep in the stuffy shack, Clare opens the door and under an unobtrusively symbolic frozen moon maintains a dialogue with the self, awakening suddenly to the idea that, after all, "I am that type" (288).

Discerning a man's silhouette—Steele's inevitable repetition and coincidence—Clare lies acquiescently until, frightened by strange movements, she quietly locks the door. The man's voice then calls for a drink of water. When Clare replies that she is not alone and has a gun, the man bangs, butts, and kicks the door until, finally exhausted, he retreats. Half-dozing until early morning, Clare then runs to "Mrs. Eccles" where three men roam about; one in uniform asks if anyone had disturbed her during the night. Not knowing why, Clare answers that she had slept soundly; the men examine foot prints around her shack and quite agree. The prints point to the quicksand pond.

On the beach with "Mrs. Eccles" later, Clare views a dead man floating in a battered dory half-filled with surf. A coastguardsman explains that this fisherman was not as tough as the other one. Steele's iron curtain comes crashing down when Clare innocently asks why the tongue of the corpse hangs out. The guardsman replies: "You never seen thirst?" (296). Although Steele did not as a rule like "radio people," he liked and allowed Max Wylie to adapt "A Drink of Water" for a powerful Columbia Workshop presentation.[8]

X *"The Thinker"*

To win back his wife, little Dummy Santos deliberately makes a hero of her potent lover. The crusty New England narrator of "The Thinker" begins his episode of the prudent, hard-working Santos with poetic echoes of Anglo-Saxon lamentation for a mid-March winter: "Ice, ice, ice, ice, ice!" And the conflict develops out of the documented drama of liberating ice-locked Cape Cod fishing boats. Three years earlier Dummy Santos—a great thinker— quietly bought a house; a year later he married wild Rosie Far- quiera, a good wife until the guano-factory worker Stinky Lorry turned her head—or nose: "Stinky has made the discovery that a great many women actually like it. Some women it seems to draw. He has seen women he was hugging, close their eyes, part their lips, dilate their nostrils, and seem to drink" (307). Why Dummy continues to fish—he fears the ocean, gets seasick, and cannot swim—remains a mystery. Rudely anxious for Dummy to leave "Portugee town," Stinky boisterously helps the crew chop the ice. As the knowing townsfolk observe the little moonlit drama, we see their admiration for free-swinging Stinky, their contempt for cowardly Dummy.

While chopping, Dummy Santos suffers psychological riot. If he leaves, Rosie goes to Stinky. If he stays, the fleet catches the herring. If he chops like Stinky, he falls into the water. If he kills Stinky, punishment comes. Finally, the answer: when Dummy asks Stinky to help him remove ice chunks with boat hooks, suspense ensues; but, instead of killing Stinky, Dummy falls into the black water. Hypnotized by fear, Stinky stirs the water with his hook while the townsfolk shout. Unconsciously, Stinky now finds himself in the water and saving Dummy. The hero carries the little cuckolded husband home, where Santos—suddenly re- covered!—congratulates his savior. (The narrator, after all, *did* remark that, while struggling with a great chunk of ice, Dummy *did* suck in his breath and swell his cheeks.)

Eager to sail south for herring, Dummy now asks the hero to look in on Rosie from time to time. But Stinky, ennobled by his own heroism, also is aware that prettier fish than Rosie swim in the sea. In the final tableau, courageous little Dummy Santos, sitting on his cuddy roof and heading out to sea, bears a distinct but tacit semblance to Rodin's monumental *The Thinker*.

XI *"Fe-Fi-Fo-Fum"*

"Fe-Fi-Fo-Fum," Steele's penultimate story in *The Man Who Saw Through Heaven*, bears a curious likeness to "Land's End," for each presents a theatrical seaside setting where a beautiful woman "plays" a deathbed scene to a love-smitten doctor. In "Land's End," however, Mary Farnoe's physician shocks his operatic patient back into a "happy ending" reality; in "Fe-Fi-Fo-Fum," the profligate, esthetic Sharon Cole tragically traps her young doctor (victim number three) in her web of emasculating patronage. The atmospheric melancholia and sepulchral tones of the death room are alleviated by jingling high jinks in the living room. There Sharon's estranged husband (a newspaperman) and her disenchanted lover (a jazzman) compare notes on their vicious cycles of idleness-guilt-drink under Sharon's spacious roof, and then they fall into animated collaboration on an "oriental" rag: "Yellow Blues."

Meanwhile, the mere presence of Dr. Jamie Butler is a psychological transfusion for the jaded "Cleopatra"; morbidly poring over treatises on anemia, she still is obsessed with hitching her monied wagon to a star—and steering it! The title and the incident of a mosquito on Sharon's pale arm make clear the analogy. A modern vampire—a less hardboiled version of Hemingway's "rich bitch" in "The Snows of Kilimanjaro"—Sharon also is an innocent soul-seeking devil, whose tempting "line" is: "Men like *you* ought to be—"

For astonished Dr. Butler, she creates a vision: "No, it's not in the workaday humdrum you're thinking of I'm interested, Jamie; not in the babies and the stomachaches of the stay-of-home. But in the adventure of the frontiers of it all—the twilight zones where biology and chemistry and physics meet—in the men that are pioneering—the men that gamble with the devil in their secret laboratories, to lose their souls or learn one little thing" (352).

In the end, each reconstructed team prepares for a new life: Sharon's two former "lame ducks" set out to conquer Tin Pan Alley. Meanwhile, Sharon's medical Adam looks out of her Edenic bedroom window and gazes at length on a fairyland in a silver sea—but, already irritated, Eve commands: *"Look at me!"*

XII   *"What Do You Mean—Americans?"*

Steele's folklorish asides on Cape Cod, English attitudes toward
the *novo português* and other *foreigners* (for example, in "Down
on Their Knees" and "The Killer's Son") become the main theme
of the weak "What Do You Mean—Americans?" With a few families on the seven-mile wrist of Cape Cod, the Brewster brothers
—Andy and Isaiah—wait out their remaining days in the country
of the old—"old houses, old sands, old men" (367). When they
die, they believe, the tide will take the Cape down under the sea.
Like old White, Fuller, and Rogers, the Brewsters also suffer
rebellious merrymaking—in Andy's great-granddaughter Molly,
who loosely keeps house.

Molly's lack of forethought and character, her slang and breezy
dresses, her "nigger" boyfriends—these, to the crabbed ex-clipper
sailors, indicate the coming deluge. When Jimmy the Greek ca-
reens up in his truck and asks for Molly, the Yankee gods just
rock their dry bones. Learning of Sam White's death, the two
defeated ones—reminiscent of E. A. Robinson's hillclimbers—plod
up Sheep Hill and inventory the cape. Between confrontations
with Manny the Lisbon who refers to "us Americans," a coastguardsman named Tony Fuller *né* Farquiera, and a policeman
named Belkar Soblievski, the brothers "rec-lect" their past law-
lessness. At home, they hear gunshots and discover Jimmy the
Greek in Molly's bed. Molly—with tousled hair, muddy shoes,
ripped skirt—rushes in and caresses the dark head. In breathless
slang she reports a successful liquor smuggling and administers
first aid to Jimmy's leg wound.

Back on Sheep Hill at dawn, the brothers regard the marsh
becoming an estuary; but Frank Silvado, the Pamet Station surfman, scientifically informs the twosome that the land really is
building up. When Andy angrily tells Silvado that soon there will
not be any folks left, the surfman echoes: "Any folks?" Brutally,
the brothers clarify: "Any—any—*Americans!*" But the bewildered
Silvado is so unconsciously assured of his nationality that he asks:
"What do you mean—*Americans?*" (396).

XIII   Meat

While *Harper's Magazine* prepared to serialize *Meat*—November to February (1927–28)—Steele hurried to Denver to visit his
ailing mother and later rejoined his wife and children in Rich-

mond, Virginia. While on their way to Charleston, South Carolina, for the winter, the Steeles visited bustling Greensboro, where the author viewed his birthplace with "moral non-recognition."[9] In Charleston, the Steeles lived in a century-old house with narrow gables and long galleys (64 Tradd Street); and the boys attended public schools. Preferring the company of a few close friends, Steele declined the many invitations from Charleston society. When the serialized version of his novel appeared, the literati of Charleston and America in general argued about its controversial thesis.

As much a moral tract as a novel, *Meat* (1928) treats the dynamic problem of the protection of the unfit at the expense of the sound. Although Steele's message in *Meat* was contrary to many American beliefs (including those of his parents), Steele concluded that his convictions, drawn from life, were honest and, in time of suppression, needed saying. To Steele, censorship was part of the "centuries-old distrust of the barbarian for the civilized man. . . ."[10] His pithy title comes from 1 Cor. 8:13, the Pauline declaration, "if meat make my brother to offend, I will eat no flesh while the world standeth, lest I make my brother to offend." Steele's preachy novel shows how one family (an allegory of national tendency) carries this notion to its logical—and absurd—conclusion. The personal "I will not" becomes Prohibition's "Thou shalt not."

Into a sane, robust, temperate New England family—father, mother, son, and foster-daughter—a second son is born, a throwback to the mother's defective Cousin Tomlin: "When Tomlin Flagg was born he had a horn, above and a little in front of his left ear. Such a thing was not unknown in his line; it had happened at least once before. The somewhat goatish excrescence lasted little more than a week before it was absorbed into the shaping skull. Thereafter it remained simply as a hairless spot on the scalp, the size of a man's thumbnail and of much the same consistency. By and by the hair could be so brushed as to cover it" (1).

Only two painful alternatives face the parents, Sam and Anne India: whether to isolate, in a sense sacrifice, the weak Rex, so that the strong, twin-like Flagg and Fern can grow naturally; whether to sacrifice the natural development of the strong children, so that the weak, vomiting child can survive. Shocked into self-immolating zealotry, once-pagan Anne India directs "pitiless care" (40) for her abnormal son. Throwing over her early conviction—"God and I are sorry, but the world was made for *well* people to live in, first of all" (74)—she lays down a morbid house-hold law: "If it won't hurt him, let him have it. If it will, keep it out of his way" (43)—and, ultimately, out of everybody else's way. Foreseeing disaster in his wife's method of fearfully gutting the house of "temptations"—unclothed children, nude statuary, discussions of war, dinner wine"—guilt-ridden Sam India protests against her Spartan nobility, her "nun's inverted ecstasy" (43), but to no avail—for his own self-doubt and his wife's Puritanical certitude defeat him.

Conditioned to degeneration, the two normal children, expelled from Eden, gradually sink into alienated, sex-warped renegades—barely salvaged after their vicious and parasitic young brother prematurely dies: "The moon gave off a particle. Out of its white-ness a red corpuscle sprang. For the thousandth of a second, with zigzag vacillation of lightning, it cast and recast about the sky. Then, spying Rex at last, unerringly, it spun down and hit him on the head (254).

Clearly, *Meat* is a bold (but perhaps ultimately vicious and self-defeating) indictment of the pernicious doctrine that the world should be made safe for the weak at the expense of the strong. Like Nietzsche, Steele shows how both the individual and the race—presumably the human race—stand to suffer from "ethi-cal" protective restrictions. In keeping with the expressions of Jesus, John Milton, Mark Twain, and American conservatism, Steele shows—if not proves—that temptation is necessary for strengthening moral fiber. *Meat*'s uneasy mixture of Darwinian naturalism and Freudian psychology seems dated today, but its problem remains— not whether the unfit shall live but *how much* shall be taken from the fit.

Steele tough-mindedly wrote: "We must be prepared to lose a lot of people who never were meant to stand on their feet."[11] Like Jack London, Steele did not allow his compassion for the weak to blind his belief that perpetuating weakness is wrong. Un-fortunately, the characters in *Meat* all are weakly drawn, even Flagg India, Steele's victimized "superman." Whether the lure of controversy inherent in *Meat*'s dynamic theme excites or not, few critics would defend its embarrassing propaganda. Flowing narra-tive alternates with argumentative points, lyric childhood fan-tasy rubs against slangy journalistic exposition, and beautiful isolated passages intensify bathetic underdistanced sermonizing. In spite of powerful and convincing scenes, the ending rings false. Drawn out, it wavers between tragic logic and optimistic luck:

unfortunately, it falls into a marketplace ending of hope for the regeneration of the strong. Gladys Graham, in the *Saturday Review of Literature,* politely wondered why Steele had so much trouble with his novel endings, "since in his short stories he is past master of crisp terminal technique."[12]

XIV   *Past Master*

By the late 1920's the reaction against old-fashioned plot destroyed many literary reputations. Steele attempted another novel and his first full-length play—both efforts unsuccessful. From 1915 to 1926 O'Brien reprinted a Steele story in all but three of his annual *Best Stories*: but so enamoured became O'Brien of new-story experimentation (and so opposed to traditional forms and O. Henry endings) that this early champion of Wilbur Daniel Steele's pioneering work did not reprint another Steele effort until 1933. Meanwhile, Steele hoped that the *Saturday Evening Post* and the *Ladies' Home Journal,* magazines which still favored strong plot, had changed their editorial ideals drastically enough to accept his grim stories. For 1928 the plot-loving O. Henry Committee chose as a prize story Steele's uncollected "Lightning," a tale of duplication and criminality.

In Charleston for the 1928–29 winter, Steele was low in spirits; Margaret was ill but taught art. On a treadmill of worry and unable now to maintain his Nantucket home just for summers, he sold it in the spring of 1929. While gathering together stories for another collection, Steele viewed Chapel Hill as the center of the southern recrudescence and toyed with the idea of making this North Carolina university town his future home. By summer the deposed master of the short story was struggling over another play in Nantucket—this time in collaboration with his wife's friend Norma Mitchell, a successful actress-playwright. The play—an adaptation of his story "When Hell Froze"—was, said Steele, "one grand desperate attempt to get myself clear of this peon-rut of short-story writing.[13] Though finished, the play was never performed. A line by the versifier in the story "Fe-Fi-Fo-Fum" seems to summarize Steele's state of mind at this time: "It's hard, when you've been so near to doing the big stuff you can't do, to get back to doing the little stuff you can" (347). Late in 1929, Harper published Steele's fifth collection of stories.

CHAPTER 6

Tower of Sand

*T*OWER *of Sand and Other Stories* (1929) includes eight narratives, seven from *Pictorial Review* and one from *Harper's
Magazine*. Only the *Harper's* story—"Never Anything that Fades"
—and one *Pictorial* novelette, *Mary Drake and Will Todd*, first
appeared in magazines following the publication of *The Man Who
Saw Through Heaven*. The other six stories the author assembled
from his turn-of-the-decade (1918-23) *Pictorial* stockpile: "For
Where Is Your Fortune Now?," "For They Know Not What They
Do," "Footfalls," *A Life*, "The Mad," and the title story, "Tower
of Sand." Diverse themes popular with Steele—sickness, awakening, superstition, revenge, love—characterize his fifth collection,
including its two novellas—*A Life* and *Mary Drake and Will
Todd*. Of those in a tighter compass, all but the disarmingly simple "For Where Is Your Fortune Now?" are marked by obliquity.

As usual, reviewers recommended *Tower of Sand*; but, as Clifton Fadiman had earlier wished in his review of *The Man Who
Saw Through Heaven*, Edwin Seaver (evidently unaware that
most of the stories in the present volume dated from an earlier
period) wished that Steele could abandon his flair for situation, for
"shifting, only temporarily satisfying arrangements" and treat
instead "raw, permanent elements"—and thus win more than "popular approval and the solemn hallelujahs of the schoolmasters."[1]
The Bookman included Steele in a portfolio of fifteen full-page
portraits of such American writers as Robert Frost, Sinclair Lewis,
Sherwood Anderson, Edwin Arlington Robinson, Thornton Wild-
er, and Thomas Wolfe; but Paul Allen censured Steele for not
writing "literature" when so many of his superior "machine-made"
stories approached it.[2]

I *"Tower of Sand"*

In "Tower of Sand"—one reviewer called it "blindly exciting"[3]

—Steele's power-of-friendship theme is strongly and clearly developed. As in "The Man Who Sat," the imaginative first-person narrator rebuilds the "catastrophe" from factual scaffolding provided by a sailor, a wireless operator. From the interplay of the sailor's facts and the narrator's figments an allegorical figure, or "humour" of the "fixed idea," emerges in the character of Uncle Two Fathom, an ex-schooner captain. Old before his time, akin to something dragged from the sea, the ragged and bony creature lives at Tower of Sand with his son-in-law, the lighthouse keeper.

Haunting the nearby compass station, Steele's ancient mariner garrulously criticizes the landlubbing wireless sailor, the system of wireless navigation, and the unreliability of marine charts. The busy operator wearily explains that Tower of Sand relays a ship's bearing to one station, which in turn provides that ship with another bearing, and that the captain then plots his own position. But, like Captain Bixby of Mark Twain's *Life on the Mississippi*, Two Fathom insists that there are a "hundred 'n' one" navigational considerations. Years before, the reader learns, the obsessed seaman had discovered and charted a dangerous two-fathom ledge. Placing humanitarianism and fame over secret knowledge of profitable halibut, the young idealist had reported Two Fathom Ledge—to Washington officials who quickly dismissed the chart. Brooding over this "obscure and fatal ledge of his like one mother to a monstrous child" (13), Miles had bestowed his chart on his best friend, Nathan, a freighter captain. But Nathan's negation of the chart had ended their friendship.

On Christmas Eve, a life-and-death wire arrives for old, dying Two Fathom. After exchanging messages with apologetic Nathan, Two Fathom guides his friend's vessel through the maze of shoals and into deep water. Although told as only Steele can tell such a story, the narrative would amount to nothing more than a popular tale of the misunderstood hero were it to end here. Little other than melodramatic effect also would be gained by Two Fathom's dying on the lighthouse walk-around, his magnified shadow making split-second flashes on the water. But this revelation is the supreme irony: after checking Nathan's bearing, the wireless crew realizes that the captain simply gave his old, dying friend a gift of charity; for, throughout the long Christmas Eve and Christmas morning, Nathan's vessel had been snug in Boston Harbor.

II   A Life

More bizarre than Nathan's expression of charity is the heroine's parting gift in Steele's incongruous twenty-thousand word mineral-vegetable epic entitled *A Life*. In this fable a child receives the gift of survival—from a *boat*! Steele's boat, akin to ghost ships and homing vessels in tales of the supernatural and the mysterious, is endowed with a consciousness (reminiscent of that "shippish other-world" of "The Yellow Cat" and the "devil woman" of "*La Guiablesse*") expressed through fusion with a sympathetic narrational voice. But imaginative sympathy, nautical accuracy, cunning indirection, and moderate suspense are not enough to redeem Steele's anthropomorphic experiment from bulky sentimentality and banality. Juvenile response to Joyce Kilmer's "Trees" is high pathos compared to the bathos of Steele's boat and child: "How desperately she would have liked to stay and keep that soft, beloved mite all to herself through a hundred sunny hours, tumbling about the dory-nests or playing grave helmsman from his high perch on the wheel-box!" (96).

But, in spite of Arthur Vance's unqualified praise of *A Life*— the greatest story to come to *Pictorial Review* in twenty-five years —the tale lacks the esthetic distance necessary today. John Masefield used a similar theme in "The Wanderer." From the beginning, when the soulful racing schooner *Independence IV* ponders her destiny of serve and be served, suspension of disbelief is strained by Steele's story. The fertilizer plant nearby outrages the ship's delicacy. Surrounded the next day by human peers, the cup-defending princess receives from an ivory-throated woman the christening "kiss of glass and wine" (45) and eagerly awaits a mast. But her coughing night watchman, soon to be deployed, bestows on her the curse of a coward's hell—and, before he drowns himself, he spits into her mast hole. With this mast-sealed impurity and curse, the ship—the calm water's bride, the swift wind's mistress—fears the violent ocean; resists her savage sail-master who calls her a "luffin' bitch" (56); and, finally, is towed into port a self-pitying failure with a broken mast. There, like Sleeping Beauty, the ship awaits her prince.

One spring day a trio approaches—an ivory-throated lady, her husband, and her husband's best friend. Identifying with the slim woman, the schooner is converted into a two-master and renamed *Helen*. Like her mistress, the schooner wishes only to idle in port, although her master would have her go to sea and leave the best friend ashore. By strength, wile, and subterfuge, the schooner fouls her mooring chain, breaks loose, and again snaps her mast. That night the husband shoots wife, friend, self, and curses the schooner for failing to carry his wife and him away to sea.

Next, merrymakers buy the coward ship and content her, until a romantic drunk, playing Columbus, tugs at her bights and sends her out past the sea gate where she hits a rock and, while luminous fish and the dead drunk float by, drowns. Purified by time and salt water, she is salvaged by old Francisco Prada. Although the fishing fleet laughs at her slender and frail lines, she suppresses echoes of her past and bravely wills to help debt-ridden Prada by becoming "stanch and blunt and gross" (81). Launching restores her memory, and love for the old man makes the queen grovel. As simple as Francisco now, she offends genteel boats and works the fishing ground. Late to market on rough seas—but first in calm—she gains the fleet's approval.

On the day Francisco's young grandson stows aboard, a storm unfolds the ship's mainsails. When the fog lifts, the dying schooner fights bayward; but her master, lashed to the wheel, is dead. Dreaming of her checkered past, she again breaks against the sea-gate rock and sinks—but not until launches sentimentally rescue the child: "She sank slowly through the water, obliquely, as if there were a crystal stairway lit by the faint, submerged irradiations of the moon. And Francisco went with her and held her wheel. And now she was not afraid. She was tired, and she slept" (114). *A Life* also seems destined to eternal rest.

III   Mary Drake and Will Todd

The next narrative in *Tower of Sand*—the two-part *Pictorial Review* serial *Mary Drake and Will Todd*—combines the form and genre exquisitely wrought by Henry James in his *nouvelles*, or long tales, about artists and writers. Beginning in end-of-the-century Far Harbor (Steele's Nantucket), the time-span stretches to thirty-one years. But most of the unity-of-place action happens within the last five years. Whitmanesque islander Will Todd (an erstwhile journalist for the Brooklyn *Eagle* and the former editor of the Far Harbor *Advocate and Sentinel*) is a slapdash handyman and versifying terror in the pillared home of classic beauty Mary Drake, who reads Shelley and Tennyson.

Neither love for Will's fascinating ambition nor for his barbaric effusions, but New England pride—in their island, in their ancestors—first compels Mary Drake to protect the self-castigating egoist from off-island ridicule. She endures both his literary fevers in the slum of his third-story bedroom and gossip about his frenzied sexual paganism outside the house. Fragments from his poetic monstrosity catch her eye:

> What man has not lifted the arms of his childhood—
>   what one as a lover
> Has not lifted his eyes to that beauty too far and too white,
> And turned him, blinded a little by it,
> And taken less? (162)

The story comes full circle when Nathan Granger, novelist turned publisher, returns to Far Harbor. (Years earlier his bride had died in a carriage accident after their visit with Mary Drake—and a silk-hatted, tan-shoed, uninvited Will Todd.) Now Granger returns to Mary Drake's neither to visit nor to propose but to publish Will Todd. Again donning his incongruous hat and shoes, Will apostrophizes the garden sunset. His masterpiece is finished, his race with fame won. He dies from consumption.

With patrician poise, sixty-year-old Mary Drake of the denouement permits the public to enter into the historic romance of her pillared house on summer Wednesdays. For all its prosaic inflation, certain memorable "touchstones" show even through Will's apprentice verse; but whether in the end he is another Whitman in free verse or simply another Sinclair Lewis T. Cholmondeley Frink in the Whitman manner is not clear:

> Don't talk to me about Beauty; I'm the lad that creates it . . .
> I am of instants: I am the two-legged emperor of instants . . .
> I am Man, . . . (179)

Indeed, Will Todd has a following, but perhaps by the host of the imperceptive. At any rate, the hero escapes the teacup lionizing briefly felt by Neil Paraday in Henry James' "Death of the Lion," and lady Mary Drake feels her high destiny fulfilled at the altar of the dead.

IV   *"For They Know Not What They Do"*

Another lady—"before the light of that worn word went out" (180)—is Agnes Kain of Steele's haunting recitative "For They

Know Not What They Do"—a story which won the second prize
in the 1919 O. Henry Awards and which Blanche Colton Williams
regarded as "fashioned as firmly as the Woolworth Tower."[4] Like
the mother in "The Killer's Son," Agnes Kain has chosen a mysterious exile for self and son rather than maintain family home
and heritage. In both stories the son's need for paternal identity
conflicts with the mother's need to conceal it. Through silence,
Anthony Brown's hysterical mother does not save her son from
the dangerous life of Bragana fishermen; but, through a hideous
lie, Christopher Kain's genteel mother does preserve her son from
the hereditary madness of the Kains. Occasionally swept by pas-
sions, Christopher finds general contentment and security in his
mother's itemized legends of the noble Kain line.

Only by chance does the fifteen-year-old boy follow his en-
trained mother to the real place (the *déjà vu*) of his "treasured
epic" (183), a seaside manse tended by an ancient servant and a
dying caretaker. Playing the role of inheritor of courtly romance
in this Thomas Hardy house of portraits, the boy finds an old
violoncello, "the shadow of some ghostly and elusive memory"
(192). The doddering servant, hardly aware of Christopher lying
on the turf the next afternoon, mindlessly (but improbably) ram-
bles on about the insane Kains and their violent deaths. Adroit
with ironic parallels, Steele has the senile servant mumble something about a cursed villager whose gossip about "dirty" Kain
blood started Daniel Kain down the road to ax-swinging madness.
This pastoral scene of uneasy knowledge Steele follows with a
storm-and-stress description of Christopher lashing madly at the
violoncello in his moonlit room. Tormented, blood-lusting, mother-
hating, he wills to make himself sick, despite Agnes' quiet
entreaties.

Realizing now the meaning of Christ's words on his father's
gravestone—"Forgive them, for they know not what they do"—the
fledgling maniac roams the woods and ancestral graveyard: "And
in that moment he knew what Daniel Kain had felt, and Maynard
Kain before him; a passionate and contemptuous hatred for all
the dullards in the world who never dreamed dreams or saw
visions or sang wordless songs or ran naked-hearted in the flood
of the full-blown moon. He hated them because they could not by
any possibility comprehend his magnificent separation, his starry
sanity, his—kinship with the gods. And he had a new thirst to
obliterate the whole creeping race of dust-dwellers with one wide,
incomparably-bloody gesture" (201).

Wielding a rusty knife, Christopher approaches the caretaker's door and views a candlelit trinity of Poesque coffin, violoncello, and lady. Confessing infidelity (choosing the chance of an exiled son's becoming mad over the certainty of a wifely reputation's being lost), Agnes Kain discloses that the caretaker is Christopher's real father. Needing some tragic birthright, the clean-blooded heir snatches up the violoncello; but, no longer a Kain, his unfrenzied music dissolves in a moonless night of purifying rain. Shortly after her son returns to school, Agnes Kain dies, unforgiven—and not until years later does Christopher, a healthy Philharmonic violoncellist, forgive her.

Unlike the heavy-handed intrusiveness of "Mr. Doctor" in "The Killer's Son," the friend-narrator of "For They Know Not What They Do" brings his story full circle by retelling the denouement in the protagonist's words. Visiting "the place" years later, Christopher explains that the caretaker never owned the Kain violoncello; that the old man had, in fact, been deaf since the age of ten; and that the villagers regarded Agnes Kain as a distinguished actress. In the end, the musician realizes that his unselfish mother played a melodramatic and sordid role to get him "over the wall" during his "nip-and-tuck years." In the light of Christopher Kain's innocent guilt and ambiguous name (Christ-Cain), Steele's biblical title culminates in still another ironic dimension. According to Steele's sister Beulah, both she and her brother knew the story's real-life counterparts—"a family in which old genes and an impressionable lad were face to face."[5]

V *"For Where Is Your Fortune Now?"*

"For Where Is Your Fortune Now?" is another portrait of sinewy love and unselfish motherhood. The story purports to exist as a non-Oedipal, nostalgic, and disarming memoir of the grown son. Because Irish Annie Ring feels that her husband Ben, presumed lost at sea these past eight years, will return "in the flesh" to the Cape one day, she declines from fear of bigamy laws to marry "the Portugee" who lives with her and young Benjie. But, after misinterpreting an ominous storm, she believes that big Ben Ring is dead and that she can marry the easy-going "Portugee." When Ben Ring appears, however, Annie's fiancé flees; but he soon returns to find an unlucky, laughing husband without ill will.

Ben and the "Portugee" spend their time casually seeking work, pitching horseshoes, and drinking beer at the local bar.

When Ben learns that his saloon credit rests not on his flamboyant rhetoric but on the good word of his hard-working wife, he again bolts domesticity. In simple faith, gullible Annie urges that Benjie accompany him so that the boy, too, can make his fortune. On the road, the *picaro* Ben uses Benjie to gain meal and money from a sympathetic farm woman. Later Benjie watches his father flirt with a lunchroom waitress. As the Ring men drift to the boxcars, Steele captures Benjie's newfound lyrical sense of wonder, of adventure, of freedom, and of love for his big, strong father.

But Benjie's love turns to hate when his father, leaving him waiting in an empty boxcar, strolls down the wooded embankment with the waitress. Through the moonlit night the betrayed boy races home. Wildly happy, Annie gathers him up and runs down the hill to the waiting "Portugee." Joyously the boy's mother weeps a refrain about his foolish return: for where is his fortune now? Unlike the complicated actions and complex figures which Peter Means cryptically recalls of his Urkey Island youth, Benjie Ring's Cape Cod domestic tragicomedy is highly effective in its fusion of simple structure, character, and language.

VI   *"The Mad"*

More simpleminded than simple is Andrew, the village fool, in Steele's Freudian melodrama, "The Mad." The omniscient narrator portrays outcast Andrew as loving children, fire, and charity. During a seacoast disaster involving fire and lost children, clumsy Andrew is rebuffed by coastguardsmen for interfering. The plot continues to develop through the pattern of rebuff. Finally, Andrew saves one baby. In the surf he sees another doll-like hand, drags up a water-logged bundle, and stupidly hands it to a wailing woman who dances for joy. Amid the long carnival of front-page disaster are newsmen and cameramen. Returning to the catastrophic scene a few weeks later is celebrity Rose Trent, one of the survivors. Andrew wanders about echoing the crowd's pronouncement: "Poor Trent." When he recognizes "Poor Trent" as the bacchanalian mother, he rushes forward—only to be rebuffed.

An awkward shifting of the point of view alters the frame of reference: Rose Trent and her husband engage in dramatic dialogue. Because she had been found *that* dreadful night hugging a water-logged doll, her wealthy husband asks his wife if she ever wanted a child. Mirthfully, the handsome woman replies no: "One long squall and mess! And think of my figure, man!" (267). The denouement focuses on Andrew, whose echo of "Poor Trent" suggests oblique paradox and message.

In Freudian terms, Rose Trent's unconscious mother-child urge is so powerful that under great stress she unknowingly played the role of hysterical mother, traumatically bereaved at loss and overjoyed at recovery. Recuperated from shock, the aging beauty represses the psychic reality of her dormant maternal instinct. Ironically, her grotesque foil, poor Andrew, also possesses, or is possessed by, a little of the *mad*. Like socially repressed Wing Biddlebaum of Sherwood Anderson's "Hands," Andrew represses his paternal instinct and primitive love for children.

VII *"Footfalls"*

Unrepressed paternal love reveals itself with a vengeance in one of Steele's great story figures, Boaz Negro, the blind Portuguese cobbler in "Footfalls." Always partial to the word's haunting sonority, Steele in 1920 elevated "footfalls" to titlehood in the often anthologized tale that he considered "extremely hard, austere, dour."[6] The self-effacing narrator of this rarefied mystery primes the reader before Boaz' perceptive mind, heart, and hearing dominate the narrative: "This is not an easy story; not a road for tender or casual feet. Better the meadows. Let me warn you, it is as hard as that old man's soul and as sunless as his eyes. It has its inception in catastrophe, and its end in an act of almost incredible violence; between them it tells barely how a man, being blind, can become almost deaf and dumb" (268). After hearing footfalls surrounding the "catastrophe" (the murder of Boaz's son), the once exuberant shoemaker grows figuratively "deaf and dumb" in his sea-town cobbler's shop during the dark nine years he awaits the peace of revenge.

A Steele feat of psychological motivation and blindman's buff, the story ends with Boaz' violent revenge. The weird fusion of introspective hero, commenting chorus, scheming villain, and sensational murder makes "Footfalls" a type of Senecan or Elizabethan revenge tragedy. A piece of information known only to Boaz—not the reader—produces the final "shock." Also, Steele "misleads" by siding first with the lusty crew that frequents Boaz' shop and then with the "rising" bank clerk, Campbell Wood, who rents rooms above the shop. All feel, however, that Boaz is too lax with his son. Boaz' repetitive protest is: "Manuel is a good boy" (275).

In the end, the reader's sympathy indeed goes to Manuel: on the catastrophic day that Boaz' house and shop burn down and bank money disappears, it is *not* the body of the "rising" Campbell Wood that is found but the incinerated and skull-crushed form of Manuel, who wears the bank clerk's charred clothing. (Conveniently, Steele makes no reference to scientific identification and postmortem.) Distrustful of abstract law and also fearful of giving the police information which might forestall the murderer's return to the scene of the crime, Boaz keeps his remembrance of fleeing footfalls secret. Cheerlessly vegetating, the old shoemaker alternates between doubt and certitude in his "blistered promontory on the shores of ruin" (288), a dark unity of place and action.

When, after nine years, the murderer does return, Boaz traps the man in the lightless shop and strangles him to death. Fearful of error, Boaz shaves the body—"the dead denuded by the blind" (298)—as horrified merrymakers break in and recognize Campbell Wood. Awed by the romantic proportions of blind justice and parental revenge, the townspeople of the old Puritan town act as both judge and jury. Quite improbably they refrain from trying old Boaz who soon regains his exuberance, his customers, and his lusty friends.

VIII   *"Never Anything That Fades . . . "*

Like "Footfalls" and other stories in *Tower of Sand*, Steele's final story in the collection unfolds an unusual parent-child relationship; in "Never Anything That Fades . . . " nine-year-old Beryl Summerhaze is a miniature version of her delicate mother. Their exquisite mutualism regarding all things virginal embraces one of widow Marta Summerhaze's new suitors; but his initial repulsion wanes into resignation. Steele's lush Edenic setting, a petal-choked summer garden at Wood Island Crossing, supports the timeless theme of conflict between the old and the new. Patient in composing his symphony of bloom, the grandfatherly gardener—who sees beauty in a fading flower—smiles indulgently on the Summerhazes:

They never saw the garden he made for them. Like the man who couldn't see the woods for the trees, they could never see the blossoms for the buds. For the triumphant full chord of his contriving, the panoply of massed and blended bloom, they seemed never to care to wait. At the full of any flower, already one petal will be drooping, already a worm may be lying secret in its heart. And so long and long before that danger, almost before it was dry of the dew of its unfolding, Marta must have it cut and carted away, giving room for another to bud and breathe its pale, beginning sweetness a moment before it, too, went into the barrow and out to the humus pile. (303)

The gardener also whittles boards—"tombstones" for Beryl's crowded graveyard under a weeping willow: "A pearl-gray elephant, passed away of a ripped felt. A wooley lamb, worn threadbare by squeezing. A blanched Pickaninny" (305).

So pervasive is the Summerhaze cult of newness that pensive John Bent, a cautious suitor, flees after ghoulishly digging up Beryl's favorite doll—one-eyed Bellinda Angelica—who has been buried by the child because Mr. Bent brought her a new one— "crisply, curling, brittly glittering" Gloria Rose (314). And because her child buried the *old* doll and not the *new* one, short-sighted Marta Summerhaze is hazy about why her male guest suddenly departs. In fact, Steele blends his floral setting with an "eyesight" motif suggesting the adage about beauty and the beholder. In the end, the lonely man—this time with "open eyes"— slips back; he is now resigned to an ephemeral relationship with the neoteric duo. Little Beryl ironically confirms Brent's unmistakable impression of genteel evanescence by professing for her new doll eternal love: "Oh, for months and *months*. Till the very end of the summer, really, Mr. Bent. Way till my birthday comes" (326).

IX   Undertow

For 1929 the O. Henry Committee reprinted Steele's "Silver Sword," an uncollected tale about an aging ante-bellum southern lady who finally surrenders her ancestral sword to the invading economic Yankee. In 1930, the year Steele moved to Chapel Hill, the southern Agrarians stated their case against industrialism in *I'll Take My Stand*. Although never identified with John Crowe Ransom and other Agrarians, Steele sympathized with their desire to retain a nation of colorful provinces rather than an expanse of dull standardization. Because Steele so loved locale and viewed the South as a living historical entity, he could refer to *Black April* (1927)—Julia Peterkin's intimate novel of South Carolina's Gullah Negro—as "the great American novel of at least two decades."[7] Accepted as an "insider" by the University of North Carolina faculty (especially by the golfers and tennis players), Steele found Pulitzer playwright Paul Green (*In Abraham's Bosom*, 1927) "particularly prepossessing."[8] Through him, Steele met Sherwood Anderson and liked him enormously.

Though impressed by the force of the nearly plotless "new story," Steele himself could not master the form. During the great depression the ratio of articles to fiction in *Harper's Magazine* steadily increased, partly because reader interest centered less on questions of individual conduct and more on problems of corporate and government policy and partly because editors, pressed for space, could not cut Steele's whole-cloth constructions. Though *Atlantic* and *Harper's* ignored conventional magazine formulas, readers of little experimental magazines regarded these cultural giants as hopelessly middle class. Of his career at this time, Steele declared: "My type of tale began to be passé and I had to try to learn how to create and live on some other form, play or novel."[9] He expanded his one-act *Harper's* drama *Ropes* into a scenario and novelette, retitled *Undertow*, which was advertised as "a thrilling romantic tale of love and sacrifice."[10] With Norma Mitchell's help, he continued work on the play version of "When Hell Froze"—and he facetiously planned a sequel, *When Heaven Boiled*.

In Chapel Hill (729 Franklin Street) Margaret Steele's health did not improve, but she managed a short trip with her husband and a few friends to Ocracoke Island, the scene of Steele's famous "Conjuh," a 1930 O. Henry Prize Story. In honor of his father, Steele participated in the dedication of Wilbur Steele Hall at Bennett College in November;[11] both of Steele's parents, in failing health at Beulah's home in the Canal Zone, were aware that their son's powerful novelette *Man Without a God* in the November and December *Ladies' Home Journal* had created quite a sensation. In his celebrated Nobel Prize address on December 12, 1930—"The American Fear of Literature"—Sinclair Lewis complained about the isolation of the American artist; and he included Steele in his generous list of vigorous, original writers who deserved recognition from the staid American Academy of Arts and Letters. Isolation, the satirist warned, drives artists to commercialism. With his fat check from *Ladies' Home Journal*, Steele bought a new Oldsmobile and gleefully drove around Chapel Hill in reverse.[12]

X   *Connecticut Playwright*

In 1931, the sky fell on Steele, and just as improbably as such things happen in his stories. His fear and trembling started when Margaret woke up on Christmas Day, 1930, with pneumonia. Their Chicago guest, Vivienne McClatchy, took over household duties until she herself suddenly grew ill. While Margaret slowly approached the critical stage, her sick visitor died of a rare disease. And, while Margaret underwent an operation in Durham, Steele shipped Miss McClatchy's body to her family. Two weeks later Steele's wife had another operation. Dazed, Steele looked on, his days and nights "spent in runnings and waitings—and not knowing what the morrow is going to bring."[13] A few days later Margaret Steele died.

After sending his sons north to Grandmother Thurston, Steele could not write for three months. Suffering Margaret's absence, changing literary fashions, Hollywood vulgarity, and his own emotional bankruptcy, Steele then joined his parents in the Canal Zone. After spending part of the summer in Nantucket with his sons, Steele revisited his ailing mother, this time (the first in seventeen years) in Denver. By the fall of 1931, he was back in New England under Norma Mitchell's tutelage; he worked on another play, but was "desperately, and worn down tired with it."[14] Slipping off to Corsica, Steele asserted by November that he was "slowly feeling like my old self."[15]

As quality magazines turned more and more to "unplotted" stories, Steele directed his efforts toward the popular weeklies and the women's magazines. In spite of diminishing markets for his best work, he won the 1931 O. Henry Prize (first place) for his humorous ghost story "Can't Cross Jordan by Myself." But the advance guard now touted William Faulkner, who was represented in the same volume by "Thrift." No teacher, lecturer, journalist, actor, editor, or publisher, Steele (through his powerful will and sense of professionalism) determined to continue as a writer. While he tried to locate stories in his mind, the mass-circulation magazines published stories from his backlog.

From London on January 7, 1932, Steele acknowledged his mother's death in Denver and wrote his grieving father: "What a terrible year 1931 turned out to be in all our lives! Poor father and poor all of us!" Then he announced his coming marriage to Norma Mitchell. Just as the father in Steele's "Bubbles" tells his daughter that he is "not much good in this world—without somebody" (98), so, too, did Steele inform his family that he could not "carry on alone," that he was "no good at it—worthless." On January 14, 1932, at the Westminster Registry Office, the forty-five-year-old writer quietly married forty-five-year-old Norma Talbot Mitchell, his "best friend."[16] Norma's first husband, whom she divorced, was Hayden Talbot, an American correspondent in London.

Soon after their marriage, the Steeles returned to the United States. They set up house at Seven Acres, Norma's eighteenth-century country home in the hamlet of Hamburg, Connecticut. No longer wanting to travel, Steele chopped wood and pessimistically wrote plays and stories. *Ladies' Home Journal* and the *Saturday Evening Post* accepted a number of stories—old and new—but *Harper's* seized upon only one. In June, 1932, the University of Denver bestowed on its literary son an honorary doctorate. When Steele's last *Harper's* story finally appeared in August, 1932, even the futuristic Edward J. O'Brien could not resist the wild romantic irony of "How Beautiful with Shoes" and reprinted it among the achievements of F. Scott Fitzgerald, Erskine Caldwell, and Katherine Anne Porter in *Best Stories of 1933*.

During the winters of 1932–33 and 1933–34 Steele and Norma pursued solvency in Hollywood; but feeling lost there, the story-teller looked forward to spring gardening and old-style writing back at Seven Acres. Paramount Studios hired Norma for a bit part in *The Woman Accused*, and Rico Studios provided Steele with "flowing gold" and "incredible anguish."[17] Returning home, he wrote stories for *Saturday Evening Post* and *Collier's*, while Norma wrote radio sketches. Together they wrote a never-produced three-act comedy about collusive divorce, *Any Woman*. During his 1933–34 Hollywood winter, Steele wrote a treatment of Philip Gibbs' *City of Temptation*; and then, returning to Hamburg, he wrote several fine stories—too grim for publication. Since writing stories seemed as big a gamble as playwriting, Steele and Norma, in September, 1934, collaborated on another comedy, *Post Road*.

XI Post Road

Written by the Steeles in one month and sold in three days, *Post Road*, under the direction of Anthony Brown, was a hit Broadway mystery-comedy. With its "grand cast," the play opened on December 4, 1934, at the Masque Theater—where *exactly* one year earlier Director Anthony Brown's *Tobacco Road* had begun its sensational run.[18] Though the Reverend Steele, senile in Denver, could not attend his son's Broadway opening, Thurston and Peter (down from Brown University) boosted their showman "Pops," who now switched from pipe to cigars. Brooks Atkinson referred to *Post Road* as a "not untalented play that refuses to make its peace with the theater."[19] The next year Samuel French published the play which ran for two hundred twelve performances on Broadway.

Post Road (1935), a one-set piece which Steele described as "folksy comedy," begins humorously at the New England tourist house of kindhearted, mordant-tongued Emily Madison. The audience, like Emily and her boarders, is at first innocent of the real motives behind the emergency intrusion of a moaning girl, a doctor, a nurse, and a chauffeur. The mysterious comings-and-goings of the four are consistent with the titillating premise that the unfortunate girl, a socialite, has given birth out of wedlock in Emily's house on Boston Post Road. For days mother and child remain incommunicado—supposedly because of the mother's shame, fright, and peril of scandal in high places.

Actually, the girl and her loyal confidants are professional criminals, nimble at the art of high-grade kidnapping. Through circumstantial evidence, Emily and the audience discover the "reality"; and the comedy then shifts to a frame of menace, evoking in the audience both commiseration for and impatience with the household innocents. Although the billion-dollar baby in Steele's happy-ending drama is never in any physical danger from the sophisticated operators, the Hayes Office refused permission for a screen version because the Lindbergh kidnapping and the Hauptmann trial were too fresh in the public mind. Retitled *Leaning on Letty, Post Road* had an enormous Chicago run during the 1937–38 season.

XII How Beautiful with Shoes

Loathing the metropolis during his 1934–35 winter in New York, Steele collaborated with Anthony Brown on a three-act stage adaptation of "How Beautiful with Shoes." Never published, the unsuccessful play opened at the Booth Theatre, November 28, 1935—and Steele switched from cigars back to his pipe after the eighth and last performance. The underlying sexuality in the story (see Chapter 7) is overt in the play. Loutish Ruby Herter elaborately sets up his and Mare Doggett's marriage bed. Among characters added to the stage version is Sil Tooker (village slut and foil to Mare) and Ruby Herter's pal Bilbo (whose lusting after Sil is a junior-league version of Ruby's lusting after the virgin Mare). Corn liquor and horseplay occupy the wedding guests who await the arrival of Mare's shoes. Reward money motivates Herter to join in the search for Humble Jewett, the escaped lunatic. Jewett first encounters Mare in her bedroom as she prepares to bathe. Amid wild festivity, a judge and doctor discuss Jewett's paranoia praecox; and paralleling Jewett's romantic abduction of Mare is Bilbo's animalistic seduction of Sil. After killing Jewett, old Wycker tells Ruby Herter that Mare and Jewett were on the "sofy." The angry Herter retrieves his bed, but he returns after the doctor assures him that Mare is still pure. As in the story ending, the awakened girl cannot now abide her coarse betrothed.

"Many a playgoer," reported *Time*, "will find *How Beautiful with Shoes* a hodgepodge of demented tommyrot. A few may see in it some of the wild majesty of such great plays of the Irish Renaissance as *The Playboy of the Western World* or *The Unicorn of the Stars*."[20] Running a perilous course along the dividing line between prose, poetry, and absurdity, the play charmed some critics, chilled others. Those touched by its poetry considered the play to be unlike the usual commercial ruck. John Chapman viewed it as no second *Tobacco Road* but as a play whose folk minds do not rise as high as the beautiful surrounding hills which lessen the human squalor. Those critics untouched by its poetry saw the play as trying to be something it was not. Expressing cool chagrin, Gilbert Gabriel described the Steele-Brown collaboration as "a coarse scramble, confused of mood, unsteady of structure, eloquent only in those lulls which come when everybody on stage seemed out of breath from sheer shouting."[21]

Again living in New York, Steele *again* gave up writing stories, but proclaimed: "It's the devil's own life, the theatre."[22] On March 17, 1936, Steele was fifty. A decade before in "Crocuses" he had written: "There's nothing to keep the human carcass well ordered, elastic, lusty, and young, like a living faith—in almost anything. And there is nothing so ruinous to the tissues of fifty as finding that faith suddenly brought in doubt" (145). Laboring under doubt and apparently buttressed by weekend parties at Seven Acres, the story writer-turned-playwright became playwright-turned-novelist. Ten years after *Meat*, he completed another full-length novel.

XIII Sound of Rowlocks

Sound of Rowlocks (1938) was Steele's sixth novel; but, more properly, it was his first and only long (343 pages) psychological mystery or detective story. Set in the isolated fictitious village of Isle Haven, lying fog-bound off the Nantucket shores, the story focuses on lovely Gay Coward and a triumvirate of the several men in her life: her friend Dr. Finnigan Harrie, her epileptic brother-in-law Humbert Coward, and her murdered husband Beal Coward. Feuding with these "all-year-rounders" and with a group of seasonal duck-hunting sophisticates are satirically individuated but authentic rock-ribbed New Englanders, "gloomy Grundys in the dark of a Godforsaken, shut-mouth, Puritanical island, to hell and gone out in the wintry sea" (35). Characters of neither faction, but still drawn into the scabrous dramatics, are a mysterious German swimmer; a state trooper (Corporal Theodore Roosevelt Ogordowski), who feels patronized by the dour natives; a veteran detective from Hyannis; and, among several other pen-portraits, a solitary Portuguese wife who accommodates the German fugitive. At the end of the novel, goodwill and communal ratiocination penetrate the red herrings of circumstance. While suffering one of his psychotic seizures, jealous Humbert Coward, it turns out, had shot his brother with the latter's own hunting gun. With the sick brother marked for medical attention, the good doctor and the good widow attain amorous rapport.

Steele's experiment, combining through stripped style a serious novel and an entertaining "whodunit," is ingenious—perhaps even absorbing to mystery addicts. *Time*, for one, viewed the marriage of genres as compatible and rated the mystery as number one of the month's bumper crop.[23] Indeed, Steele complicates his long conundrum handsomely—not only by additional homicides (and methodically shifting points of view, which achieve a sense of simultaneity and of information persuasively withheld), but by transcribing without narrational intrusion trooper Obediah Coffin's comprehensive and involved notes of detective Wykk's interviews with sundry witnesses and nonwitnesses, reliable and unreliable. But, for the serious reader of quality fiction, *Sound of Rowlocks* does not ultimately satisfy.

Too often "flesh-and-blood" characters detract from the jigsaw-puzzle plot, which, in turn, draws attention from the delicacies of affection and psychopathology. Had Steele managed to fuse more of the simply balanced elements, this different work perhaps would command some critical attention. But as his mystery novel stands, the case rests.

XIV That Girl from Memphis

After the Steeles' dismal 1937-38 New York winter, they took a six-month, suitcase trip to Europe; but they returned (sadly) to Hollywood the next winter. From 1938 to 1945 a trickle of Steele's third-rate, machine-made stories appeared in such women's service magazines as *Good Housekeeping, Woman's Home Companion,* and *Cosmopolitan. Atlantic Monthly* published only two distinguished Steele stories—"Isles of Spice and Lilies" (February, 1940), a complicated psychological story which Steele wrote in 1929, and "The Dark Hour" (September, 1940), a timely reprint of his powerful German-menace allegory which had first appeared in *Atlantic* in May, 1918.

While working on *That Girl from Memphis,* begun in the spring of 1941, Steele also revised a pile of rejected stories and plays.[24] World War II profoundly disturbed his "adventurous procession of the homely hours."[26] Although his early eye trouble returned and his hearing became impaired, he self-consciously joined the auxiliary police. Because of his position in a defense plant, Thurston was deferred from service; and Peter, discharged from the navy because of eye trouble also, became a radio editor. After the novel, Steele planned to work in a nearby glider factory; he felt ashamed to be "so damned well off."[26] Instead, he took a flying trip around South America for *Cosmopolitan.*

Worn down into making surrenders to the new Doubleday editorial board, Steele agreed to have Evelyn Wells doctor his long novel, which he had originally entitled "The Story of Beulah City." *That Girl from Memphis* (1945) is the first of Steele's four romantic novels dealing with the American West, none of them strictly "Westerns." More than a decade before this book, Steele had declared: "The wild West has been cheapened and exaggerated, and its real drama has yet to be written. It will furnish material for really great novels, such as have made American home life distinctive."[27] Indeed, interest in the literature of the American West is today at an all-time high.

Steele's first Western novel follows the stormy careers of two people and a city. In 1889, Garnett Cannon (an innocent Kansas orphan) and Bertha Lea Birdwarden (a beautiful Memphis prostitute)—both young, daring, and stubborn—survive a drunken Apache raid on their westering party, fall in love, and gravitate to Beulah City, a raw mining town on an Arizona silver lode and a frontier settlement destined to a life as brief, flamboyant, and violent as other western boom towns. Under melodramatic conditions, idealistic Garnett discovers Bertha's past and refuses to marry her. Later he fights and accidentally kills her rich husband. Garnett the tenderfoot, now a boxcar fugitive, gains a reputation as the "Kansas Kid," legendary hero of a popular sentimental ballad.

Heiress to a mining claim, Bertha builds a great brownstone house, harbors a crew of down-and-outers, and tries to gain respectability and social prominence. But her past, her old acquaintances, and other events frustrate her ambitions. In time, serious-minded Garnett, "an American Parzival,"[28] works his way through a Methodist seminary, returns to Beulah City, and involves himself first in soul-saving and then in public service. Action between the star-crossed lovers plays on an attraction-repulsion theme. When soldiers arrive in the mining camp to quell incipient riots, Garnett (now an earnest miner and union organizer) accidentally throws a homemade bomb and kills six men—which brings him a sentence of twenty-seven years in jail. During this time of rapidly shifting values, mining leaves Beulah City, coyotes prowl the deserted streets, Hollywood exploits the legend of the Kansas Kid, and Bertha reverts to brothel values. In 1930, pardoned Number 2009 returns to the once-fabulous but now ghostly Beulah City. After a series of Rip Van Winkle shocks, he and sinful, heart-of-gold-fire-and-steel Bertha settle down in her aging brownstone house.

Lauded by most newspaper reviewers, Steele's best seller deserves some sort of *Prix d'Ennui* as art, for most of the two-hundred-thousand-word novel is inflated, formless, and uneven. Even critic Gay Wilson Allen, who viewed the book as a "contribution toward an understanding of American folklore, mores and social history" and as a study of vulgar social forces in America, admitted that the novel is "so continuously and industriously thrilling that it ultimately becomes tiresome."[29] With "soapbox" regularity, Steele's "comeback" melodrama trudges garrulously from one overwritten tragedy to another.

What preserves this ramble through the Old West from classification as a true "Western" is Steele's labored treatment of character and place. Just as in *Sound of Rowlocks* Steele tried to fuse the modern novel and the mystery, so in *That Girl from Memphis* he tried to meld the historical novel and the popular Western. Thus his characters—not only hero and heroine, but promoters, gamblers, shady ladies, honky-tonk keepers, cowmen, miners, outlaws, poets, and magnates—all have more than one dimension. And Steele's treatment of massacre, shoot-out, flood, boom, bust, and other standard regional fare is closer to frontier reality than are the inanities of the stereotyped Westerns. In fact, the dull, empty, unthinking aspects of western life are equally treated, but without much distinction. Ideas are simple and complicated rather than clear and complex. Lacking a controlling symbol or an inner order, the profusion of colorful details overwhelms the reader who survives the creaky style. His, yet not his, Steele hated the "damn book."[30]

CHAPTER 7

The Best Stories

W HILE the author's name was still fresh, Doubleday published the central book in the Steele canon: *The Best Stories of Wilbur Daniel Steele* (1945). Of the twenty-four stories in this volume, thirteen had appeared in the five earlier collections: "For Where Is Your Fortune Now?," "The Woman at Seven Brothers," "Footfalls," "Out of the Wind," "For They Know Not What They Do," *"La Guiablesse,"* "The Shame Dance," "The Marriage in Kairwan," "From the Other Side of the South," "The Man Who Saw Through Heaven," "Bubbles," "Blue Murder," and "When Hell Froze." The eleven stories never before collected were written between 1918 and 1934, but several of them were first published in periodicals *after* these dates— most notably Steele's brilliant "Isles of Spice and Lilies" (written in 1929, but first published in *Atlantic Monthly* in 1940).

Besides this story and the superb "How Beautiful with Shoes," Steele's finest collection includes "The Dark Hour," "Can't Cross Jordan by Myself," "Conjuh," "In the Shade of the Tree," "The Body of the Crime," "A Bath in the Sea," "An American Comedy," "Due North," and "Survivor." Steele and Henry O'Neil chose the two dozen selections for *The Best Stories* from more than two hundred possibilities. As testimony to the author's narrative acumen, the volume contains five O. Henry Prize Stories, seven O'Brien Best Stories, and one *Harper's* Prize Story—but this honoring of his work was not Steele's criterion for inclusion.

Reviewers naturally hailed the publication (which ran the gamut of Steele's themes and locales) as a literary landmark. Writing in the *Yale Review*, Orville Prescott regarded Steele as not only an astonishing virtuoso, but as America's greatest living writer of short fiction. Not even Hemingway, Caldwell, and Miss Porter, stated Prescott, "so combined productivity with excellence."[1] Highly readable, sometimes dated, these stories reveal the merits and defects of the Irving-Hawthorne-Harte-James-O. Henry-London-Wharton tradition in which Steele wrote. However much Steele's highly individualistic stories differed from others, all in the tradition were constructed similarly. None gave off an aroma of psychotic reportorial maundering. Realistic details and masculine ingenuity made Steele "half a realist, half a wonderful storyteller."[2] Although such "popular" contrivances as suspense, conflict, pace, climax, surprise, and irony operate even in most "art" stories, they function in Steele on an unfashionable level of intricacy. His tough-minded reversals are on the other end of the tonal spectrum from, say, William Saroyan's childlike sentimentalities. Steele's weak and fallible heroes, even those who overcome environment, seem for the most part locked in particular grimness. Yet his *respectable* characters, as Edith Mirrielees suggests, are "worthy of respect."[3]

I *"The Dark Hour"*

"The Dark Hour" is a short allegorical story or sketch with no more "ado" than dramatic shipboard utterance between a restless doctor and his dying patient. Through the venerable form of the "debate" on morality and politics, Steele builds a terrifying, simplistic vision of eternal strife between the forces of good and evil. Because of its historical parallels and prophetic overtones, the story (originally published in *Atlantic Monthly* in 1918) was reprinted in *Atlantic*'s September, 1940, issue. Returning to America, the two cardboard "position" figures allude to the great war (symbolized by the doctor's uneasiness in the dark night) and to the war's aftermath (symbolized by the patient's focus on a bright star). Victory, the doctor knows, lies ultimately with the Allies; but he is troubled by Germans who "won't play the game, won't abide at all by the rules of logic, of common sense. Every day, every hour, they perform the impossible. It's like clockwork. It's like a rehearsed and abominable program—" (201).

With eyes on his star, the expiring patient believes that just in *holding* back the German military machine, the democracies perform the impossible. But the open societies lack what the militarists possess: "A dream. We've dreamed no dream. Yes—let me say it! A little while ago you said 'nightmare,' and I said 'dream.' Germany has dreamed a dream. Black as the pit of hell—yes, yes—but a dream. They've seen a vision. A red, bloody, damned vision—yes, yes—but a vision. They've got a program, even if it's what you call it, a 'rehearsed and abominable program.' And they know what they want. And we don't know what we want!" (202).

The uplifting republicanism and puritanism of University Park no doubt fostered in Steele his repulsion of autocratic Germany and possibly attracted him just before and after World War I to the ideal of universal socialism. Highly effective later as anti-Fascist propaganda, "The Dark Hour" suffers somewhat as art. The author's understandable but vigorous sympathy with one side of the argument tends to corrode esthetic distance. Unlike the best medieval debates, here no need for a judge exists. Particularly obtrusive near the end is the patient's inorganic, fairly detailed rhetoric about his visionary father, a notorious barricade radical, who fought the black dream with a white one. When the radical's son affirms the need of new absolutes—"democracy as a wild, consuming vision" (204)—the skeptical medical man views the idea as utopian.

The shipboard interlude ends with the bewildered physician pacing the rolling deck (perhaps a metaphor of his soul's dark journey) and hearing from the deathly shadows the whispered refrain: "That's a bright star, doctor" (199). Included in the *Best Stories of 1918*, "The Dark Hour" seemed to O'Brien a superb exception to the mass of sentimentalized or denatured war fiction.

II *"How Beautiful with Shoes"*

Of Steele's stories the most anthologized—perhaps Steele's greatest story—is "How Beautiful with Shoes." Here the hoary triangle of hill-billy fiction—highland girl, local suitor, influential stranger— moves on a high level. The main conflict—highly suspenseful, highly sensational—is between a cloddish Carolina girl and her platonic abductor, an asylum escapee. The crazy man's adoration of beauty, his tortured memoirs of war on ugliness, his tender recitations of sensuous love poetry—these things the terrified girl hardly kens; but shortly after the outsider's violent death, she awakens emotionally, her accustomed world crudely clashing with her new feelings, strange and wonderfully delicate.

Steele achieves unified suspense through two plot cycles, and the second round of action magnifies the first. Each cycle dramatizes (1) the girl alone, (2) the girl and her betrothed, (3) the girl and the psychotic, (4) the girl and her betrothed, and (5) the girl alone. In both cycles, the girl-and-the-psychotic scene is central, symmetrically balancing a pair of scenes before and after. The quality of the daft man's monomania, the ritualism of oak-and-willow Appalachia, and the subtle shifting of the omniscient point of view from the girl's vantage point contribute to the naturalness of Steele's bold formalism and the parallel actions.

In the first plot cycle, Mare (Mary, Amarantha) Doggett, setting down her milk pail, drifts toward the masterful sound of whiplash. Halting his mules, tobacco-chewing Ruby Herter calls his betrothed and commandeers a few rough springtime kisses, "his hands careless of contours" (275). Interrupted by a carload of roughnecks, Ruby joins them in a search for an escaped "loony"—the restless stranger wearing baggy overalls who shortly afterward, in the presence of the insularly deaf Mrs. Doggett, extravagantly greets "Amarantha in Carolina" with courtly praises and pastorally bids her come with him. Fearful but instinctively calm in the vicinity of ailing animals, Mare bides her time until the searchers return and jail the loony in the courthouse.

Wearing her new, pinching, two-dollar shoes to impress her inquisitive neighbors, Mare and the others learn from Older Haskins, cousin to Mare's dead father, that the "loony" is Humble Jewett, a college man who had taught "somethin' 'rother" in an academy a few years back until he had half-killed his principal with an ax and had almost strangled a girl. Sickened and shocked, Mare steps outside; from a rise, she discerns the courthouse on fire (like the earlier blood-red sunset); and she pities the trapped animal inside. But, having killed his guard and fired his trap, the monomaniacal Jewett eludes his pursuers and returns to the Doggett farm where he gently leads the numb Mare into the night hills. There, passing into full-scale fury, he smashes another door—this one to the cabin of old Wyker, Herter's cousin.

In the empty cabin, Jewett pours out Cavalier and Renaissance poetry—Lovelace's "Amarantha sweet and fair—Ah, braid no more that shining hair . . ." and the anonymous "O western wind, when wilt thou blow . . . ." He also expounds upon his mission—how Christ had commanded him to lift a sword against the hypocritical and lustful academy principal who had forbidden the teaching of Solomon's "Song of Songs" as human love poetry. When the unchurchly and embarrassed Mare responds to Old Testament eroticism with "Aw, no, don't talk so!" (287), Jewett's ecstasy

turns to anger, and he confuses Mare with one of his victims—
the principal's dormitory wanton. After Mare pleads that she is
not "Blossom"—simply "Mary"—the remorseful Humble Jewett envisions her as the Mother of God and, painfully exhausted, falls
asleep in her arms. At dawn, whiskery and whiskyish Wyker
intrudes upon the beatific scene and shouts to Mare—"Come
jumping!"—and with both barrels, he shotguns sleeping Jewett.
Back home, Mare repeats to everyone—doctor, mother, betrothed
—"Go 'way! Lea' me be!" (294).

Before her awakening, Steele's finest story heroine was simply
a healthy animal, one not much different from Donna Salisbury
of "Six Dollars." Symbolically "Mare" to the hill folk, the milkmaid is described as a "broad-fleshed, slow-minded girl" (275).
Her bovine satisfactions consist of relieving distressed animals,
stepping barefoot on clods, accepting rough handling from her
mulish suitor, and not puzzling about things. Before her captivity,
she is a weather-vane of a girl—wooden and without personal will.
Perhaps from her moody father (who named her "Amarantha")
she inherited a set of rich emotions—undeveloped because of his
early death and her mother's deafness.

Responding more to the manner than to the substance of the
crucified platonist Humble Jewett, Mare insists that she is neither
the sinful Blossom of reality nor the courtly Amarantha of Jewett's
imagination; she is simply "Mary"—not the insane idealist's Virgin
Mary but simply milkmaid Mary. Only later, cloistered in her
room after the madman is killed, does the disturbed girl puzzle
over whether only crazy people talk and run the way Jewett
did: "But what fright does do in retrospect is this—it heightens
each sensuous recollection, like a hard, clear lacquer laid on
wood, bringing out the color and grain of it vividly" (292).

Transcending her accustomed reality, she recalls poetic fragments, senses the delicious mystery of the self on a mythic
moonlight run: "Mare ran. She ran through a wind white with
moonlight and wet with 'the small rain.' And the wind she ran
through, it ran through her, and made her shiver as she ran.
And the man beside her leaped high over the waves of the dead
grasses and gathered the wind in his arms, and her hair was
heavy and his was tossing, and a little fox ran before them in
waves of black and silver, more immense than she had ever
known the world could be, and more beautiful" (293).

Her unbraided hair symbolizes spiritual liberation, and her
tight shoes signify bodily restraint. Out of her puzzling and in-

articulate self-awareness (ironically the result of her harrow-
ing experience with a maniac), Mare exchanges the repressed
feelings and animal sensuality of rustic puritanism for the expressed feelings and angelic contemplation of romantic platonism.
Her willful "Lea' me be!" is a type of Joycean epiphany, for to
reveal her precious new feelings to heavy-handed Ruby Herter
(ruby-hurter) would be to cast pearls before swine. (The story's
opening sentence shows the primitive Mare feeding a raucous
sow.) Indeed, her awareness of inner beauty and exterior ugliness creates puzzles not easily solved. As a foil to the swinish
Ruby Herter, Humble Jewett (humble Jew) is a type of esthetic
rather than moral savior. Steele's treatment of Jewett places "How
Beautiful with Shoes" among such modern classics of the "sick-
story" genre as Sherwood Anderson's "Adventure" and "Hands,"
Conrad Aiken's "Silent Snow, Secret Snow," William Faulkner's
"A Rose for Emily," and J. D. Salinger's "A Perfect Day for
Bananafish."[4]

III   *"Can't Cross Jordan by Myself"*

Reviewing *The Best Stories* in *The Weekly Book Review,*
DeLancey Ferguson singled out "Can't Cross Jordan by Myself"
as a farcical ghost story so well done that "it leaves one wonder-
ing why Mr. Steele has so seldom allowed himself to be funny."[5]
The omniscient narrator of this 1931 O. Henry First Award sets
the mood with a tongue-in-cheek description of a Charleston
ghost that each month unerringly swings from a giant oak, a
feat which "argues a strength of spectral character beyond the
common run" (296). Steele's humorous ghosts—southern "mars-
ter" and folk "darky"—haunt their stately manorial rooftop at
Indigo Landing. To this incongruous situs, Steele adds the classic
interplay of Deep South local-color attitudes in Judge Percy
Legare's affectionate wrath and Sam's "Maussa Percy" dialect.
When ghostly Judge Legare balks, for example, at his own un-
controllable moaning, the Negro volunteers: "Oh, but Maussa,
excusin' me, a ghost bound *obliged* do that, when he *han'tin'* "
(306). Ceaselessly, the Judge calls Sam such endearing names as
"blockhead," "baboon," and "gallows-meat."

In this Dixie comedy of errors the Hindu medium to Legare's
"damn-Yankee" spiritualist daughter-in-law informs him that his
own servant murdered him. Sam guiltily explains that, discharged
by the Judge's termagant daughter-in-law, he had hidden in the

abandoned smokehouse, mistaken his whisky-seeking "Maussa" for a "ha'nt or hag," struck him with a timber, and made him a ghost. Finding Legare dead, good neighbors had run down Sam (southern style), introduced him to the hanging tree, and made another ghost. Although the fraternal Judge forgives and comforts his conscience-stricken servant with massive verbal abuse, Sam (no uppish "swamp nigger") chooses to remain eternally with "Maussa" as a hanging ghost instead of crossing Jordan as a snow-white angel by himself.

When alive, Legare, a stubborn atheist, had regarded the psychic carpetbagging of his daughter-in-law as so much "damnfool table-tapping flimflams" (296); now Legare, an atheistic ghost, does not discern Sam's "Hebben" across the "Ribbuh." Echoes of the "spooky" opening close the tale: "There are still ghosts in Charleston. Doubt as you can, you can't doubt some of them. You can't doubt the one that, incorruptibly, at the hour of the rising of the midnight moon each month, hangs by its neck from the Hanging Tree" (315). Although Judge Legare's baptismal flights resemble the picaresque spirituality of Mark Twain's Captain Stormfield, the Judge's sights are surrealistically grotesque. After visiting his cousin's oblivious household, Legare returns to his own mournful deathbed scene; and then, to collect his perturbed thoughts, he speeds first to a decayed Georgian manor (a knife-stabbed hostess intrudes) and then out to Colorado (a prospector's ghost dines on his own spectral fingers).

Under its amusing surface, "Can't Cross Jordan by Myself" contains satiric motifs—the ruinous effect of industry and commerce on the Old South, the misplaced scorn of Yankee professionalism for amateur spiritualism, the ridiculous loyalty of black for white, and the flabby notion that immortality is attained without struggle.

IV *"Conjuh"*

In "Conjuh," Steele dramatizes the debilitating effects of ultracivilization on the natural wellsprings of human power. His vital locale is a sea-island plantation off South Carolina. Into this relatively loose and "natural" story of a prodigal daughter Steele skillfully integrates details of flora, fauna, smells, sounds, living conditions, and folk customs of Gullah Negroes. After many years as Mademoiselle Delia Manigault, famous exotic dancer of the Parisian art world, cinnamon-skinned, has-been Delia Manigo

(with a king's decoration in her pouch of jewels) staggers home
one hot spring to her mammy's makeshift Carolina cabin. Fever-
ish and coughing blood, alternating between English and her
native patois, between dreaming and waking, working and faint-
ing, Delia finds herself the next evening unconsciously responding to the powerful rhythms of gourd and keg. After dancing on
the firelit marsh bank, she clings to the earth in a happy state
of rebirth.

This story is timely and profound. Before Delia reenters the
great cycle of nature, Steele unfolds her artificial past not through
her quaint Gullah speech—"What I come here foh, hoe weed an'
crabgrass, or listen to field-nigguh sweetmout' all mawnin'?"
(325)—but through her distorted dreams and nightmare of pursuit and falling. One sophisticated dream is a page from the
Parisian *Le Matin* praising the talented children of jungle and
slavemarket, especially the "infinitely subtle gaucherie" of Delia
Manigault whose art prefigures "the measure of the morrow's
dancing of a hundred million feet" (326). *Le Matin*'s prediction
and Steele's description of Gullah dancing do indeed coincide
with today's gyrations: "Men, women, girls, and boys, all ages,
they danced, each one solo, sufficient to himself" (330). In its
ironic use of dancing as one aspect of cultural diffusion, "Conjuh"
suggests "The Shame Dance," but it fortunately lacks the strained
coincidences of the earlier story.

V   "In the Shade of the Tree"

However, the story succeeding "Conjuh"—"In the Shade of the
Tree"—depends for its catharsis much less on locale (perhaps a
New England river town) than on a crudely contrived confrontation between two old men—the long-suffering husband of a
woman *just* deceased and her *just* returned one-day lover of many
years before. Saintly Leander Killen, interrupted all his desperate
married life by the ringing bell of his invalid wife, no longer feels
numbness, let alone love, but private and positive hatred. At one
point, the philosophical narrator shifts the point of view from
Leander to representative neighbors who foreshadow other neighbors and who validly regard the eccentric old man who is
weeding his garden (perhaps symbolic of wasted life and dying
love) as a loving martyr. Disturbed by the bell's silence now, the
conditioned husband reenters the neglected house and finds his
wife dead.

Many neighbors come to administer to the shocked Leander, who bolts into the garden. While trying to recall something that could resemble what the neighbors call "loss," the struggling Leander hears the ghostly clang (a curious neighbor); and he again bolts, this time down to the river. There a loquacious and ruddy ancient mariner spins a yarn of early sexual conquest, on this very spot, with a big-bosomed young wife named Marjorie whose husband was on a trip. Confused and angry, Leander threatens the old sailor, but he is unable "to make it momentous, that dirty little pebble in the great white flood" (347). The climax is reached via jumbled fragments breaking through Leander's habitual repression: a clean kitchen, the birth of a son, Niagara Falls, parental pride, the son's accidental death, mourning, the lovely garden. In the death chamber, Leander (now in the shade of the tree of memory) imagines the corpse as "still and white, full-breasted and young and beautiful" (348); falls to his knees, and (to the neighbors' relief) weeps. Under the circumstances, the painfully ironic reversal—the husband's pent-up hatred releasing itself in the form of love—is well prepared, appropriate, and psychologically, if not morally, understandable.

VI *"The Body of the Crime"*

Again Steele exploits the process of recollection in "The Body of the Crime." Having always suspected his father of some horrible crime, young Daniel Kinsman, especially fearful after his mother's death, runs away from camp and home to an empty house. For days he willfully summons the remembrance of things past, and these memories are reconstructed heavy-handedly by a self-conscious narrator:

> It is impossible to tell it, by a tenth, adequately. For by the very mechanics of telling, nine tenths of the formlessness is lost; fragments, released from the peculiar bedevilment of the nightmare, inevitably fly together. Detached words, fractional phrases, flickering by, flitting back again; before they can be written here they must needs have formed themselves by some degree into sentences, no matter if the sentences are forever changing something of the forms. As, for instance, in the one, "Dan (Tom), what are you doing?" followed by, "*Tom*! (Dan!)." (365)

The associational crime Daniel reconstructs: "Murder!" Returning from a Canadian hunting trip Daniel's father and his family doctor find the boy digging under the pear tree. The few old bones there, he learns, are those of his mother's favorite pet, a dog long ago bludgeoned to death by his father. Not knowing that the dog was hydrophobic at the time of the bludgeoning, Daniel's hysterical mother screamed *murder*—a word which registered on the mentality of the babe-in-arms and remained for many years a source of anxiety.

VII *"A Bath in the Sea"*

For all of its hard-boiled, slice-of-life dialogue and detail, "A Bath in the Sea" indirectly reveals the circumstances surrounding the drab existence of a blonde piano player. Steele's use of a flat, choppy, slangy style reflects metropolitan barbarity and nightclub shabbiness, in contrast to the appropriate alteration of tone and style at the end when Marty Martello (Martha Matthews) returns to her father's refined seaside home of good music, good books, and good food. Her return occurs after the accidental death of her blind, defective son (whom she loathes) —seven painful years after the death of her husband, Martello, at Bellevue Hospital.

The particular conflict in this atypical Naturalistic story with its strong illusion of uncontrived cause and effect centers on Marty's desperate need to acquire by the next day fifteen dollars more for payment on her life insurance premium. After thwarting one bandleader's advances, she winds up with only five dollars and no job. Because she now pleads for "anything," her grubby agent sends her to Harlem: "How would they know? Don't kid yourself; they've got dinges up there blonder'n you are, dearie. Don't let 'em see your fingernails too close, that's all; put on plenty of perfume and call Bendigo 'Mister.' Goldstone enjoyed himself. He thought he'd call her bluff. 'Well, you asked for it!' " (375).

In the scorching night club, Bendigo ironically ridicules her capacity to "pass" for white: "You're nigger here, baby, and your going to play nigger" (376). The tympani player, an animalistic Gullah Negro, lasciviously repeats: "I lub yalluh galls" (376). As soon as an elderly white drunk passes a ten-dollar bill to the frightened piano player, Marty tries to exit; but Bendigo insists on pooling it. In the process of close persuasion, Bendigo inspects her nails and hair and recognizes her as a white intruder, but Marty, surrendering the money before he can close his office door, rushes outside and into a taxi with the elderly drunk who ironically blubbers about his first date with a "nigger." After he passes out, Marty extracts ten dollars from his billfold and by dawn is safe in her tenement apartment. Later at the crass insurance office, the babysitter calls: Marty's little boy, foreshadowed as vulnerable, has fallen into a manhole and died.

The climax, however, occurs three days later when Marty, home among grass, white fences, horses, and wicket sounds, bathes in the night sea, the great tides rolling her over, physically, psychologically, and spiritually cleansing her entire being. This great single effect and symbol of purification and renewal Steele carefully prepares with motifs of interruption each time the urban Marty tries to wash or bathe. Also, her city behavior—strong will, sense of duty, sexual ethics—becomes understandable when aspects of her upbringing unfold.

VIII *"An American Comedy"*

The physical and psychological clash between white and black in "A Bath in the Sea" is more fundamental but no more dramatic than the contrasting rivalry of Steele's next story, "An American Comedy," written ten years earlier. But the conflict between Caucasians focuses on an illiterate Latin immigrant's son who strains to outdo an unruffled Anglo-Saxon Son of the American Revolution. Steele's frank depiction of the superiority of older, aristocratic virtues over newer, democratic vices is refreshing; but its quaint finality relies, after all, on the absenteeism of old aristocratic vices and new democratic virtues.

From democratic Iron River slums, crude, amoral, and envious John Ruffo has pulled himself upward as a contractor into the ranks of the vulgar new rich. Now each dusk the derby-hatted cigar-puffer emerges from his chauffeured limousine and, gazing down upon the growing city, proudly measures the construction of his magnificent Centennial Bridge. His vision of Iron River matches Babbitt's Zenith: "He saw towers growing, factories and tall office towers cutting up through twilight first with skeleton blades of steel, then overclothed with granite, brick, and glass" (387).

Recognizing the baggy-trousered water-colorist below the unfinished span as a former schoolmate, John Ruffo hails him and ironically adds, "You built it, not me!" (388)—for the moneyed contractor vividly recalls how schoolboy battles with this despised David Winter, a frail, solitary "dude," initially drove him to succeed. Once he fought David Winter and won. Once he wore a newer shirt to school than David Winter. Once his gang waylaid Winter, enabling Ruffo to date (eventually marry) David's girl —cool, still Celestine Lafarge—who lacked the "brighter allurements of such as Rita Nero and Myrtle O'Hare" (395). Surrounded once by glittering wedding presents, John had laughed at David's niggardly gift from college: Celestine's penciled profile.

Yet in every case, John Ruffo senses, the defeated Winter somehow had snatched the victory. But lacking a tradition of fair play and refinement, John Ruffo seems, in Spencerian parlance, "infinitely better fitted" (393) than David Winter to win the battle for the new America. With a fairy-tale motif Steele underscores as false the assumption that bootstrap-pulling *really* makes one taller: when Ruffo takes his future bride to Fairyland, for instance, the narrator stresses the appearance-reality dichotomy: "The ferry barge, jeweled with lights. The Ferris wheel, the car whirled high against the summer stars. The nectar of soda fountain, the ambrosia of hot-dog stand. The triumphant hug. The wild, strong kiss in the dark" (396).

The story shifts back to the heights, where the poetic colorist shows the solid builder a few landscapes, including one of Centennial Bridge completed. When patronizing John Ruffo notes the three-year-old date, David Winter admits that dreaming a bridge takes time. Climactically, the deflated contractor connects this tweedy visionary with the familiar architectural firm on the centennial blueprints: "Hartley, Blake & Winter." Thus the pattern of foiling caricatures ends as it begins, with a lucid espousal of the ultimate worth of David Winter's—and Steele's—aristocratic tradition. No Dreiserian tragedy, the lambent conclusion to this American dream indeed makes it an American comedy.

IX *"Due North"*

The somewhat protracted "Due North" treats a transcendental order of love ironically. To popular romantic courtship (boy-meets-girl, boy-loses-girl, etc.) Steele adds the dimension hinted in his navigational title—*Heaven*. But Steele's dramatic supernaturalism owes nothing to the traditional permanent abode of the redeemed or to depression Hollywood's gold-clouded stairways of escape. Rather, his Heaven in "Due North" is a temporary extension, a coherent materialization, of earthly desires; but this coherent materialization is experienced *as one's familiar earthly existence*. Steele's final irony results from the juxtaposition of the supernatural and the natural, a technique central to "twilight-zone" science fiction. While the spirit of Steele's heroine sails due north through the cold beautiful night with the husband and the son of her heart's desire, her poisoned corpse lies on a morgue slab in sweltering Atlantic City.

To this double-edged conclusion the narrator details "cowardly" May Coberly's thirty-odd years of failure. As a seventeen-year-old delegate to a Methodist convention in Ocean Grove, New Jersey, the panic-striken Iowan had fallen in love with a charmingly rugged sailor bound for Atlantic City. But true to form, she ended up in a hospital in eastern Iowa, with appendicitis, relatives, and a horn button from the sailor's jacket. Two years later willowy, star-crossed May had married the transcendental sailor's foil—boyishly handsome Sylvester Templin, the church baritone; but May was an unhappy bride. Trying everything from carrying an opera spear to handling hide, Sylvester finally devoted himself to musicology while May, losing faith, obtained a clerkship to support her husband. At thirty-one she heard a union-hall lecture on immortality through progeny, from which she emerged a modern woman—hard, strong, independent, gladly barren.

Steele captures the quality of her hell on earth:

All she knew was that horror came to her as she lay there in the dark beside him and couldn't sleep. Finally she couldn't help herself, she lifted on an elbow and stared at the grayness his whiteness made in the gloom. There was something unnatural, unhealthy, unright. Between a boy of seventeen and a man of thirty-four there ought to be a difference, in mind and in flesh. Either a thing is alive or it is dead. If a mind is alive it doesn't quit. If flesh is alive it changes, grows, grows older. If it's dead it's only so much meat, and decays—unless you want to keep it on ice. (413)

But pregnancy soon added to her torment, and the relationship between "Syl" and his musical companion, Fred, carried homosexual overtones. When May saw a newspaper photograph of bearded Eric Abernathy—her sailor on the train—with his wife and son on their boat in Atlantic City, following their adventurous Arctic expedition for the Smithsonian Institute, she fainted;

but she recovered in time to give food money to Sylvester and Fred, on their way to a radio audition. After the duo's success, May no longer felt obligated to live. She withdrew most of her bank money and planned an anonymous suicide in Ocean Grove, but she impulsively chose Atlantic City. While waiting for the ebb tide, she destroyed traces of her identity. On an offshore float, she waited. As a storm approached, she took the poison tablet from her weighted wrist bag and plunged into the ocean.

Her marine struggles mesh with a series of happy implausibilities under which Steele the writer bares his head: her rescue by Abernathy & Son, her mistaking the horn button for the poison pill, and her graceful recuperation as the one and only Mrs. Abernathy. In the end, of course—button, button, Steele has the button—for May there is only poison, death, rigor mortis, and a little bit of the author's theoretical heaven.

X *"Isles of Spice and Lilies"*

The central figure in "Isles of Spice and Lilies" also hails from Des Moines, Iowa—Steele's symbolic seat of dullness. Printed in *Atlantic Monthly* in 1939, this tantalizing Freudian jig-saw puzzle had been written by Steele ten years earlier. Cured of scarlet fever, teen-ager Merrill Margatt suffers from amnesia. The source of his subconscious hysteria, according to the San Francisco hospital psychiatrist, lies in Merrill's disguised dream of a signboard, white friars, white rocks, killing natives, Thursday, a bell, darkness, three gray sisters, spices, wages, death, and the moon. Merrill's recording medical angel warns, "That guy in the subconscious has a thousand dodges, double meanings, association hookups, far-fetched puns" (439).

Although his own sailor clothes and tattoo are unfamiliar, Merrill does recall his visiting father. Together they return to Des Moines where Merrill undertakes his labyrinthine adventure in dream interpretation. *Déjà-vu* scenes at home underscore his blank wander year. Working as an apprentice toolmaker, he marvels over his skilled mariner hands and over his forgotten voyages to spicy South Sea islands. He even turns chaotic dream into ordered poetry—reminiscent of John Livingston Lowes' fascinating reconstruction of Coleridge's imaginative process in *The Road to Xanadu* (1927). Pedantically encouraged by a mousy librarian, Merrill decides that revisiting his isles of spice and lilies is the only cure for his amnesia. His father, willing now to finance the trip, volunteers the information that he had left home the last time because of parental strapping; but Merrill decides not to accept the money and to repeat the identical pattern, choosing as modes of transportation foot, thumb, tramp, schooner, junk, and proa.

Additional *déjà-vu* experiences on the outskirts of nighttime Des Moines throw light on his distorted psychic dream: "Native White Rock Fryers Killed Every Thursday" reads a familiar poultry sign; a bell sounding over a bakery door suggests the three Grace sisters; the smell of spice there—cinnamon, nutmeg, coconut—is unmistakable. Rushing out the rear door, he recognizes another sign rising against the moon; and he then confronts the youngest Grace sister, Lily, vaguely married now, plumper than last time—the time his irate father retrieved and whipped him.

A truck to Dubuque, a job in Minneapolis sorting old clothes, a job in Albuquerque carrying a tattoo-parlor signboard—Merrill finds enough linkage in his traumatic past to rule out his South Seas venture. Bidding the wanton Lily goodbye, the boy races home under a clear sky. Like "The Killer's Son," this story deals with self-identification; but on the level of allegory, "Isles of Spice and Lilies" dramatizes the artist's shaping and synthesizing of the welter of perceived fragments into a form of beauty, ironically steel-knit.

XI   *"Survivor"*

As disguised autobiography, Steels's last effort in *Best Stories* is appropriately placed. "Survivors" deals with a Last Mohican among the tribe of artists in a world of shifting tastes and generational barriers; but under variety's surface Steele dramatizes the universal creative urge. His artist-hero Dobson, an elderly sculptor-teacher and "ex-lunger" in raw, conservative Denver, dreams of his Oxfordshire boyhood and Montmartre bohemianism. A type of the dedicated artist (a well-trained Israel Atwood), he fastidiously completes for the state capitol his great Indian figure —"Arapahoe"—commissioned by impatient Philistines: "How could they comprehend that, so long as a last knuckle wanted a least wrinkle to make it right, though it might seem good enough in their eyes, in the artist's the whole creation remained but an attempt, and a foiled one, so much dead clay? They seemed not to realize that it was to last a great deal longer than they. But they were like that, forever building things in a hurry so as to be able

the sooner to tear them down, in a hurry to build newer ones"
(455–56).

With Philistines, the staunch artist lumps lovely, vigorous
Mary Shannon, a student *fond* of studio atmosphere—"not the
hard fashioning of a beautiful thing" (455). Dismissed from
class one spring night, the girl kisses Dobson's symbolic bald-
ness and retreats with the governor's dilettante nephew. Visiting
Mary's studio home at Mrs. Shannon's request that winter, Dobson views the *blobs* of his former student—so like the Reverend
Diana's in "The Man Who Saw Through Heaven"—and feels
humiliated. By the following spring Dobson completes his monumental Indian and angrily recommends that the exhibition committee not include among the various exhibits the inanities of
Mary Shannon. But the function of the governor's nephew is
clear: he prompts his uncle to override old Dobson's veto.

When the Philistines naturally attack the girl and her distorted
bronzes, Dobson quixotically defends his former student with his
emblematic bywords: "Good! Push on!" Later his sense of fool-
ishness and dishonesty is intensified when arty riffraff cheer-
fully drag him into a dirty eatery. There he interprets Mary
Shannon's warm thanks as sarcasm. Leaving these deluded youths,
Dobson notes that his "Young Circe"—a window fixture of his
friend's art gallery—has been replaced by Mary Shannon's egg-
and-cylinder Indian, "Survivor." Although praising Dobson's art,
preferring it, in fact, to modernist Epstein, Villon, and *Shannon*,
the owner points out that, after all, these are new times.

Back in his workshop the aging sculptor (psychologically blind
to the essential similarity between his own anti-Romantic Montmartre rebellion and Mary Shannon's anti-Impressionistic Denver rebellion), defensively, creatively, envisions a companion
piece to his capitol figure. Not unlike himself, "Arapahoe Mother"
will be bowed, burdened, but unbeaten. All the story's momentum
—all the healthy spirit of artistic madness—powerfully projects
itself into the old survivor's final inner direction: "Good!
Push on!"

XII   Diamond Wedding

During the next five years, a kind of escapist neo-Gothicism
grew out of World War II neurosis and the natural reaction against
Realism—literature not far removed from the order and psychological implications in *Best Stories*—but Steele himself again

turned to the Western novel. *Diamond Wedding* (1950) appeared three years after A. B. Guthrie's big-selling *The Big Sky*. Although Steele's historical fiction also treats the vanishing-wilderness-and-Indian theme, it lacks Guthrie's striding style and easy humor.

Diamond Wedding is the involuted life story of slow-thinking, slow-speaking Gowd Skinner who, even after laborious contemplation, usually makes grievous choices. Found floating down the Ohio River, passed from hand to hand, the westering orphan (at fifteen) hooks up as muleteer with Frémont's disastrous Fourth Expedition (1848) across the frozen Rockies. After Utes save Gowd from starvation, he lives among them as "Gun Giver" and (like Guthrie's Boone Caudill) takes on "Injun-ness." Later this white Indian runs into mythic Jim Bridger and becomes himself a type of the Old Scout. Gowd Skinner serves in Chivington's New Mexico campaign but not in his Sand Creek Massacre. After the Pike's Peakers dig in, the solitary, semisavage, semicivilized mountain man Gowd self-reliantly carves out another career—that of rancher. Twice he happens upon the same pretty girl; but, unlike Bertha Birdwarden of *That Girl from Memphis,* Hope Wheelwright of Rhode Island is a gentle, well-bred missionary's niece.

For a year Gowd and Hope find themselves snowed in at a deserted mountain cabin. When Gowd leaves the shelter to hunt down a midwife for Hope—the couple married in the sight of the Lord—he comes back with "Doc" Harries, who alone of the Skinners' later family and friends shares the secret of their unconventional alliance. Through grueling years on their heavily mortgaged Colorado mountain ranch, ramrod Gowd and stalwart Hope rear three sons and a daughter. The males defect to mining camps and city lights, and the female is seduced by a hired hand—paralleling the earlier cycle of flight, wilderness, and promised land. In 1919 the materialistic Skinner descendants popularize their political-economic power by exploiting in public pageantry their pioneering ancestors' sixtieth anniversary with a "diamond wedding." Dispatched by a yellow tabloid to dig up some sensational dirt on "Mr. and Mrs. Rocky Mountain," columnist Gertrude Lowe ("The Gertie Lowe Down") discovers their common-law marriage; but she turns in a twenty-one-word scoop: *"They may be a bunch of bastards, but they blew those two old people to the wedding of their lives tonight"* (309). Hope and Gowd die in 1922.

In allegorizing the movement from frontier and rural democracy to urban and suburban oligarchy, Steele obviously values the earlier "American Dream." His vernacular history, all within the span of human memory, provides a solid basis for evaluating change. But, however fascinating Skinner's character and era, Steele's wood-chip style (at best a reflection of his hero's laconic taciturnity) mars the book's readability without enhancing its esthetic qualities. According to Coloradan Dale L. Morgan, writing in the *Saturday Review*, the novel is "thoroughly characteristic of the people, the history, and the habits of mind which makes the Coloradan a separate species in the genus Westerner . . . "; but the story is "set forth with almost maddening deliberation, all cross grained in its structure, with a prose so knotty and gnarled that one must occasionally back away to grease the teeth of one's understanding before the meaning can be sawed out."[6]

Among others, Walter Van Tilburg Clark, a brilliant novelist of the American West, also regarded Steele's points of view as "distractingly various," his style as "forced," and his conception as "jerkily episodic."[7] In Clark's opinion, *Diamond Wedding* leaves the impression less of a novel achieved than of one sketched: Steele never settled on whether his narrative was to be a larger, more detailed novel (which would have fulfilled a larger intention) or a surprise-ending story (which is all that the diamond-wedding device justifies). In truth, Clark discerns clearly, for Steele's rugged novel *was* a compromise—one springing from his surprise-ending tale "Diamond Wedding," a story which had appeared in *Woman's Home Companion* twenty years earlier.[8]

CHAPTER 8

Full Cargo

STEELE closed his forty-five-year literary career with a substantial but anticlimactic book of previously collected and uncollected stories—*Full Cargo; More Stories by Wilbur Daniel Steele* (1951)—and two more tedious Western novels—*Their Town* (1952) and *The Way to the Gold* (1955). *Full Cargo* includes nineteen stories first published between 1915 and 1939, most in *Harper's Magazine* and *Pictorial Review,* the rest in *Collier's, Ladies' Home Journal, Saturday Evening Post,* and *Seven Arts.* Eleven tales had already appeared in Steele's five collections before *Best Stories*: "The Yellow Cat," "A Devil of a Fellow," "Ching, Ching, Chinaman," "Six Dollars," "The Thinker," "Fe-Fi-Fo-Fum," "Autumn Bloom," "Sailor! Sailor!," "Never Anything that Fades," and "The Body of the Crime." Collected for the first time are one novella—*Man and Boy*—and seven stories: "The Black Road," "A Way with Women," "Renegade," "The Gray Goose," "By Appointment," "Two Seconds," and "Brother's Keeper."

As summed up by Mary Ross in the New York *Herald Tribune,* these imaginative stories display vigor and suspense; each exhibits Steele's technical expertness and, because of its clear imagery and essential truth, lingers in the memory.[1] John Brooks of the New York *Times* referred to each story's underlying truth as an "idea core," as a working out of conflict between characters, while the neutral author merely throws over his tale "a light mantle of poetic insight."[2] Because these stories are not within "easy commuting distance of everyday life," and because, like Conrad and Maugham, Steele clamped his characters into strange situations and watched them wiggle toward nobility, degradation, or death, *Time* labeled him, at sixty-five, "a reactionary and flavorful old fogy."[3]

But Clark Kinnaird, in the New York *Journal-American,* wondered why Steele was not given more recognition as a literary artist: "Men are knighted in England, or elected to the French Academy, for less."[4] Again, *Time* expressed the climate of opinion: "At his best, Author Steele can stir a jigger of irony, a dash of adventure, a spring of the exotic and a pinch of mystery into a tippling good yarn. At his worst, he makes the tricks of Fate look like the hoked-up tricks of the trade."[5]

I   *"The Black Road"*

Full Cargo leads off with a prodigal-son story rich in biblical allusion. Its title—"The Black Road"—connotes the route to spiritual death. Dull, guileless Homan Ederly—in appearance like the stupid brother of "Blue Murder"—does not see the scriptural parallel of his butchering a fatted calf on the day his quick-witted runaway brother returns to the family's general store in the Connecticut Valley. A bit of dialogue on cheese—period-piece Yankee twanging between Papa Ederly and a pair of lady customers from the station-wagon set—sympathetically exhibits the narrow Ederly morality.

Into this routine conservatism enters youthful Davie, a transcendental *picaro* who charms away his years of absenteeism and repays familial love with the promise of millions: his esoteric road lore will transform the fusty general store into a garish supermarket. Using his father's good name in Hartford, Davie sets the machinery of alteration in motion that evening by extracting some expenses from the till box—new clothes for himself, his mother, and his future sister-in-law, Jenny. Having earlier gleaned the combination of the store safe, he cautions his family about ubiquitous thieves.

The low-tension supper scene heightens as Davie restively watches cars whiz by the backwater sideroad. Verbally, he creates a crossroads restaurant (like one in the West); and then, fondling Jenny, he invites her to the movies; politically, he remains floored after bovine Homan knocks him down. The prodigal son then assures the others that just three hundred dollars could make him a million out West. His parents confer, and then, one by one, the family congregates in Homan's room. All is exposed to Davie—Papa's store safe, Jenny's engagement ring, Momma's coffee-can bank. Their conviction is that "Given money, wheedled money, is always back to wheedle again. With taken money it's a different story; it goes and stays" (15). Deliberately, the family leaves its valuables unguarded and leads Davie into temptation. Tension mounts; and then, as alternatives disappear, tension crumbles. The misgiving, crushed family darkly ponders Davie going down the black road to make his millions. This stark scene powerfully ends the story.

II "A Way with Women"

"A Way with Women" also moves on a statistically low plane of probability, but the issue it projects—the uneasy alliance between the figurative and the literal—is authentic. Lost in the Carolina hills during a hunting trip with business friends, middle-aged Lothario B. J. Cantra circles around hysterically until dusk; he stumbles upon a moronic milkmaid in a tobacco-road setting. Cantra's third-person, limited point of view unveils a man lusting for his partner's modish wife. Swaggering into the barnyard now, Cantra resiliently views a dumb wife and her "deef" husband as real "Primitives." As in "How Beautiful with Shoes," Steele splendidly renders the sense of hill life, contrasted here with Cantra's city.

Unable to sell stubborn Jess Judah the idea of riding him to town tonight, Cantra amuses himself by suavely eyeing cloddish Cath over cornmush, watery greens, and oily side-meat. When late that night the country dolt brings a blanket out to Cantra's wagon-bed, the city slicker warms to the "cult of the outdoors." Rosie Santos' attraction to Stinky Lorry in "The Thinker" prefigures B. J. Cantra's attraction to Cath Judah: "This primitive stuff, by God it got you. Even the barn-stink. Like learning to like anchovies" (138). His claptrap about tropical isles, Paris, and Hollywood ruffles the girl's composure not a whit. After he fondles her five-and-dime necklace, however, she lets the big stranger kiss her flaccid lips before returning indoors.

This dusk-to-dawn pastoral resolves itself when Cantra wakes up to hoof sounds under the jouncing wagon. Cath, carrying her new man off to "furr" Hollywood, doles out commonplaces—enough to tell Cantra (and the reader) that sometime during the night she had murdered her husband in his deaf sleep. The effective moral irony lies in Mrs. Judah's stupid crime's incriminating Mr. Cantra in poetically just punishment. Without excessive straining, the title now reads: "Away with Women!"

III   *"Renegade"*

Another antiwoman story, "Renegade," stresses the camaraderie among prisoners to whom all evil is feminine. Steele focuses on car-thief Harry "Kid" Kendall, twenty-three, educated to hate all women by three prison mates—strong-arm Cardigan (who killed his woman and her lover), burglar Chapel (who had his informing sweetheart murdered), and the freakish Planck (who raped a provocative blonde). A prison parson's epilogue of the foursome reveals how Cardigan and Chapel escaped in 1928 after Planck had protectively "soaked up lead like a blotter" (143).

Five months later young Harry is released from prison, but in a few days he returns—this time to the death house: "Even the death house may not be hopeless, but it was hopeless for him. Had he slain a man in anger or a woman in passion—one never knows till the last instant what a governor may do. But this that he had done was wanton, and it was not less than matricide. You will say, but he was an orphan; how then kill his mother? And I will repeat, it was not less than a kind of cosmic matricide" (144).

The parson faithfully renders Harry's idiomatic statement of motive. Ailing after his release, Harry finally located his two escaped jailmates and joined their highjack attempt. As a "hitch-hiker," Harry forced the truck driver of contraband liquor into a side-road guarded by Cardigan and Chapel. At the rum-runner's legitimate moving and trucking business (ironically, next door to a state-police station), the tough driver brushed Harry aside; but the driver's mother invited the fever-ridden Harry inside. Improbably, she fed him, bedded him, and informed him that her son ran liquor; that men planned to highjack his truck; and that the quiet farm of her dreams depended on this last load. Although the orphanage graduate resists change, the old lady's invitation to live on the farm as her "second" son had a strong appeal. He offered to drive the truck down the back road.

The tempo of Steele's story quickens as Harry's accelerated fever, speed, and indecision combined to force his pursuing mates into a dreamlike crash—a contrast to convict Planck's earlier protection. When troopers later stopped Harry for speeding and inspected his truck, they found only plow parts. Back at the trucking business, Harry realized that the real liquor truck had gone and that the old witch on the porch was laughing at him. Like the car crash, Harry's murder of the old female confidence artist is esthetically distanced. In clipped, confused argot, he simply

tells the parson that he had to stop "that devil from laughing"
(158). Harry's epilogal hate *before* his murdering of the old lady
contributes not only to suspense but to *that* which the prison
parson sought—understanding.

IV   Man and Boy

The novella in *Full Cargo—Man and Boy*—first appeared in 1931
as the two-part serial entitled *Man Without a God* in the *Ladies'
Home Journal*. The recondite quality of Steele's finest king-sized
story no doubt is due to its twenty thousand words which is somewhat unwieldy for conventional short-story anthologies. The title
Man and Boy emphasizes the duality or divided nature of Homan
Exum Macy, a southerner torn between boyhood Fundamentalism
and manhood Scientism. In the end, old Homan Macy (Human
Race) reverts to the muscular faith of his youth; and, like Steele's
man who saw through heaven, he creates God in his own image.

To convey biblical images woven into the texture of Homan's
material world, Steele resorts to a genre of Impressionism hinted
in his episode MOVING PICTURES, which shows "how life looks as
it goes past your eyes. Fluttery, blurry glimpses. A shutter that
sticks or a film that breaks, leaving you befogged in another
darkness" (188). Impressionism reinforces Steel's structural mo-
saic of nineteen titled vignettes, each dramatized in the form of
philosophical apostrophes to Homan and others.

With brilliant economy Steele assembles the ante-bellum
world view. Sharp selectivity next dramatizes the conflict between
religion and science. Not religious belief, but the preacher's attention to Homan's sweetheart, turns the youth, ironically yet convincingly, against Fundamentalism. Through sound psychology
and backwoods terror Steele paints the reactionary forces directed
against Homan. The dialogue between Homan the "scientific" man
and Homan the "religious" boy—the dialogue of the divided self
—is a highly effective motif. Steele develops complication plausi-
bly by making the skeptical Homan inspire the town youth,
including his sweetheart, to seek fulfillment beyond the South.

In keeping with the tale's episodic structure, time contracts.
Homan becomes the grizzled town drunk; and the town itself,
now industrialized, becomes the seat of drawling Babbitts who
speculate on the grand question of football scores. Particularly
moving in this "anti-progressive" social satire is the cemetery

scene where lonely old Homan asks two young lovers—grand-children of his youthful friends—if they have the *faith*.

The final vignette—GOSPEL TRAIN—unites with the first vignette, and Steele again draws the ante-bellum world view of red fields, cotton, stars, and Methodist meetings. Finally, Man and Boy are *one*; the self is no longer divided. At the spectacle of Homan leading the young lovers into church, an old woman shouts: *"Looks like Homan—'tis Homan—infidel, sot, and sinner, come through the power of Christ crucified, come to Grace before he dies!"* (204). The montage of Homan's remembrance, present condition, congregational voices, statements by the lovers, and explanations by the godlike narrator concludes in a confrontation between Homan and the Father. In the end, Homan wants to see biblical literalness, and he wants to sleep on the Bosom of the Lord. Because of its persistent theme and fascinating technique, this novella deserves more readers.

V   *"The Gray Goose"*

Thematic entrapment and technical epiphany in "The Gray Goose" suggest certain stories in James Joyce's *Dubliners*, particularly "A Little Cloud." But, unlike Joyce's Little Chandler, Steele's Maynard Ross ironically discovers quasi-salvation in the metropolitan quagmire. "The Gray Goose" presents two landscapes: one, urban reality; the other, pastoral illusion. Twice Steele has Maynard Ross prepare to flee New York and fail to do so. Both of Maynard's adventurous decisions, years apart, stem from his bizarre vision. Neither tattered reverie nor fragmented dream, his recurring premonition comes sharp and whole; but Steele provides suspenseful inconclusiveness: Maynard pictures himself carrying a gun and a goose across a pale marshland solitude, sees himself climbing an isolated hill, sees himself about to rap on a house door—then real city sounds shatter the vision.

Maynard's first decision to escape the city came at age twelve when, to save his soul from the snare of a counting house, he begged to sail before the mast. Maynard's attitude, a youthful Conradian longing for elsewhere, Steele had earlier defined in " 'Romance.' " But, disenchanted by the captain's patronizing invitation to board the ship for a repair voyage to the Jersey shore, the guilty boy returned to the unattractive morass of widowed mother, dwarfed sister, younger brother, and office stool. Maynard's second decision to escape came when he was a successful middle-

aged alderman, free to roam now that his mother and sister had
died. But, before boarding a steamship to faraway places, he made
a romantic gesture out of his "twenty-five masked and buttoned-
up years" (283) by refunding money from the inflated sale of his
property. At the dock, however, a lawyer baited him with the
fact—Steele perhaps is excessive here—that the opposition had
entangled Basil, Maynard's younger brother, in false murder
charges. Accordingly, Maynard returned to the political arena, this
cyclic structure an ironic commentary on the disparity between
Maynard's strong aspirations and his stronger sense of duty.

The last section, part three, reveals sixty-year-old Maynard Ross
running for mayor. Reputed to be honest and tough, he also is
popular among the electorate because he is "always there." But
fleeing the net of political well-wishers and his vindicated brother,
he loses himself in the New York election-day throng. When a
package falls from a truck, the "cosmic conspiracy" against Maynard begins. Pressed on by the night crowds, he closes in by train
and by taxi on the terrifying correspondence of name (if not
address) on the package: Mayne Ross, Broadview Terrace, Moor-
church, New Jersey.

Steele's description of Maynard unwrapping the goose, holding
it by its legs, and trudging with his cane across the Jersey meadows up to the hill house door of his alter ego is an eerie study in
atmospheric gray, old age, and the uncanny convergence of illusion and reality. After delivering the fowl to Mrs. Mayne Ross,
the weary traveler pauses to read the fence placard. Evidently the
absentee husband is Maynard's double, a happy-go-lucky, peri-
patetic jack-of-all-trades, a specimen of the duplicated self that
the actual Maynard might have been; but Steele aptly keeps
Maynard's double out of the action. From the terrace Maynard
views the spectacle (couched in O. Henryesque terms) of the
election signals on the *Times* building: "Not Bagdad and Babylon
rolled in one city was ever so bedizened, so deviously and adven-
turously peopled, so fabulous" (295). When an observing Jersey-
man amicably remarks that Ross leads and that it would be "some
fun to be in that guy's shoes tonight," Maynard vehemently agrees
and walks on in tears.

Thus this warring ages-of-man story and myth of duality ends
ambiguously. On one level, Maynard's tears of recognition symbolize his sorrow in not being in Mayne's shoes tonight; on
another level they symbolize Maynard's joy in being what he is.
But, less simply, the tears complexly symbolize Maynard Ross'

ambivalence—the mixed emotions of the divided self. In this respect, Steele's double-purpose use of "tears" resembles Robert Frost's deceptive "sigh" in "The Road Not Taken." Heroism may be found even under the suppression of destiny.

VI *"By Appointment"*

"By Appointment" concludes with the anomaly of an exiled Romanoff living off a poor cockney widow. Royalty-worshiping Mrs. Panpipes, the widow of this bittersweet comedy, first sees Andrey Alexis, the noble soldier of the czarist era, after she breaks from the London crowd to pick up the frightened exile's fallen glove and to return it through his limousine window. Uncustomarily, she patronizes the local pub before returning to her lodginghouse; through cockney interior monologue, Steele characterizes her rehearsing the one-upmanship nonchalance with which she will relate the thrilling experience to her gossipy neighbors.

Later, influenced by newspaper opposition to Bolshevism and nihilism, she suspects that her two new, wealthy male lodgers, who occupy both her flats, are secretly destructive. As she shops lavishly for "Mr. Johns" and his man "Webb," her interior monologue mixes comfortable complaint and cockney proverb; and "the tide of her morals flowed and ebbed, as her courage ebbed and flowed" (301). When "Webb" brings jeweled ladies upstairs to "Mr. Johns" one night—and Constable Brightonbury just outside the door refuses to come in and "fetch" them—Mrs. Panpipes feels particularly scandalized. From the stairway she recognizes the unmuffilered "Mr. Johns" as no other than Andrey Alexis, another of Steele's monumental coincidences.

Assured by journalistic "experts" that the scattered Romanoffs soon will return to Russia in triumph, the Englishwoman now worries about her future solvency and pledges not to gossip about "'Is 'Ighness" under her low roof. In time, she exchanges the joys of revelation for those of secrecy—but labors over numerous versions of a window sign which she will exhibit the moment her majestic guest leaves: BY APPOINTMENT—TO THE ROYAL HOUSE OF RUSSIA. With grim humor the intruding narrator interprets nightly sounds outside the lodginghouse as foiled assassination plots and the landlady's frenzied sign-making as a race against the Romanoff return.

But as the years pass, Andrey Alexis' thousand-ruble drafts pile up in her bureau drawer; by decade's end, he walks the nearby park in shoes purchased by his landlady, who is now living on another unprepared coincidence—a small weekly inheritance from her sister's estate in Leeds. Even when some girl tosses a penny to the shabby flirt on the park bench, the old duke shuffles back to the lodginghouse and royally nips the hand that feeds him. Mrs. Panpipes, unable to cast him out, gives the sick man porridge and sends him to bed. A story of a widow's destiny (an old woman supporting an old man), the symbolism embraces modern history (the victory of communism over privileged monarchy) and extends into myth (the eternal movement of the wheel of fortune). Ironically, even in defeat the crown weighs on the people.

VII *"Two Seconds"*

In contrast to Steele's O. Henryish roads-of-destiny stories, "Two Seconds" implicitly argues the power of a "chance instant" to redirect one's life—in this case, tragically. The mysterious disappearance of an Oxford scholar resolves itself twenty years later aboard a transatlantic liner. The "outside" narrator (on the faculty of a western college which hired but never employed the young Englishman) learns from the "inside" narrator (a passenger named Abbott) of Hugh Cleric's torment and death in a western village. Steele used this technique of detached coincidence with the same degree of implausibility in "The Shame Dance," but Hugh Cleric's hypochondria, prefigured in the pathology of young Ray in "The Woman at Seven Brothers," is psychologically dramatic and clinically accurate.

A type of the dedicated scholar dreamer, Hugh Cleric has delusions of failure. After receiving his master of arts degree with honors, he suffers a nervous breakdown and views his position in western America as alternating between illusion and reality. Sounding like Conrad's Preface to *The Nigger of the Narcissus*, the inside narrator (who nursed the scholar in an obscure western town) insists that his shipboard listener "see" Cleric clearly, see how the scholar idealized the western college—"unless I can make you see that, I can make you see nothing" (323).

"Two Seconds" nicely balances Cleric's internal and external conflicts. While playing deck shuffleboard on his boat trip to America, the recuperated scholar glances up by "chance" and sees "something" fall overboard: "And for that half of an awful wink that pinkness seemed, either to the eye or the imagination, to have folds like legs and corners like tiny clutching hands"

(324). Later, unable to read in his stateroom, Cleric hypersensitively hears people in the passageway. For his soul's sake, he informs the searching group that he saw something fall overboard, perhaps a lavender scarf (symbol of Cleric's illusion). Desiring only self-effacement now, he views joking about scampish children, explanations of how the searching will be conducted, and maternal grimaces as Machiavellian conspiracy to break him down.

Under the strain, Cleric cracks; but he maintains his secret. After embarkation, he confesses to the mother that he saw her child fall overboard; but the scholar then flees. At the train station he confronts a talkative American who holds forth on the TRAGIC SEA PUZZLE in the newspapers. Seeing his photograph in the paper, Cleric flees to a shabby hotel, leaving his luggage on the train. When doctors later quiz him, Cleric, thinking them plainclothesmen, cleverly twists his answers and convinces himself that he only dreams. On this note, the story ends—Cleric's later deathbed confession to the "inside" narrator already prefigured in the opening. Cleric's sudden disappearance dramatically extends the story's lost-child theme and ironically comments that one can be lost on land as well as at sea.

VIII   "Brother's Keeper"

In "Brother's Keeper" Steele attacks moral hypocrisy through his characterization of near-pathological Joe Louden, a founding father of a growing Colorado town. Middle-aged widower Louden sublimates his sexual drives into righteous censorship. One spring night a year after his wife's death, Louden watches with alternating excitement and depression vibrant youth exiting from the town's picture theater that is located in a building Louden leases to a Jew named Geltmann. There Louden bids hello to young Irma Cass; and his eyes follow her to the car of Jerry Pola, the new clerk in Elkhart's hardware store: "As Irma slid under the wheel, getting in, Louden saw white at the top of her stocking, the skirts were so short they wore these days" (339).

Accepting Geltmann's invitation, Louden enters the theater for the second show, watches nudgings and proddings in the dark, and perspires heavily during an oriental seraglio scene. Longing to protect the innocent but unable to cast out his own libidinous images, he arranges for Ed Cass and Elkhart to view the picture privately; but his friends remain undisturbed. The next day Louden begins his personal cleanup campaign: "While he had dreamed he was still planting a green spot in the desert it had already flowered and gone over into decay" (343). At the grammar school, he is shocked to overhear Ellie Cass (Ed's youngest daughter) utter a "filthy word" to a playmate. Seizing the child, he escorts her home for punishment; but he wonders first if he himself should not spank her bare skin in his office.

Later Louden makes Geltmann show him a "Bible picture" with Babylonian dancing girls, after which, thrilled, he militantly dismisses the patrons. After frightening Jerry Pola home, he happens upon weeping Irma and, his arm around her plump shoulders, walks her home. When Mrs. Cass informs the men that Irma is pregnant, Louden picks up Pola, drives him out to the prairie, horsewhips him, and then points him to the next train depot. Tranquil in his scourge of indecency, God's "instrument" returns to the Cass home and compassionately offers to marry Irma. "Yes, it was more thrilling to give than to receive" (352).

But the next afternoon "charitable" Louden sadly learns that Ed Cass has permitted Irma to join Pola. Meeting Elkhart, the undaunted fanatic talks of running for mayor, of bringing in the Ku Klux Klan, and of cleaning up the town. Elkhart presses his old friends to join him on a jaunt to Denver. In the train's smoker, Elkhart, slightly intoxicated, relates humorous "remember stories" about young "heller" Joe Louden. When Elkhart recollects Joe's own shotgun wedding, the self-righteous hypocrite points out that in those days, after all, things were different. Slyly, Joe Louden drinks from his friend's flask and reasserts that the town belongs to them, not to foreigners.

IX Their Town

Compared to the high point of *That Girl from Memphis*, Steele's Doubleday novels steadily declined, both in quantity and in quality. His third Western novel, *Their Town* (1952), reveals a cross section of Colorado life from 1895 to 1930. The action centers around the once-booming, silver-mining town of Argentite on the western slope of the Rockies; around a Methodist Episcopal school called Centennial University; and around the elegant Windsor Hotel in Denver. (Historically, the town could be, say, Aspen; the college, Steele's University of Denver.)

Compelled by a deathbed promise to his washerwoman mother (a drunkard's widow) to become a millionaire, orphan Hube

Spooner plods his way through school and college—a foil to wealthy Boston dude Cabot Cunningham, whom Hube regards as a "shallow jack-a-dandy" (41). As tortoise to hare, Hube beats Cabot (who gloriously trips) in the famous Centennial Mile Run; later the oxlike Hube also marries loyal Kentucky Holm—childhood friend, campus sweetheart, and daughter of Argentite's last well-to-do citizen. During their thirteen years as man and wife, news of quixotic Cabot Cunningham (expelled in his junior year for smoking in the library) oddly influences their lives. To make his fortune—by saving Argentite—fumbling Hube clutches at economic straws, but he proudly refuses money (even will-money) from his father-in-law. With sweat as collateral, the mulish opportunist plunges into such enterprises as growing prunes on peach and apricot stocks, manufacturing composition leather, and setting up a hotel home for the tubercular. Townspeople view the taciturn plodder as gambler, businessman, idealist, or fool; meanwhile, Hube's devoted wife sustains his epic struggle.

In the end, however, curious reversals appear in *Their Town*— a book which the *Library Journal* described not quite accurately as a "folksy, warm-hearted piece."[6] Before Hube's childless wife dies (just a few days after Cunningham's death in Mexico), she exposes to her friends at the Windsor Hotel her long and terribly lonely married life. In time, the Scrooge-like town savior, personal and communal prosperity now ashes in his mouth, sees his image in a strip of burned, wasted, shameful land in the very center of Argentite. Assumed deceased by his alma mater (that idolizes the memory of freedom-fighting Cabot Cunningham), aging Hube Spooner finally realizes that the noble Bostonian intentionally tripped himself in the mile race. In a final reversion, Spooner imposes his ghostly name on the town that would overshadow him by turning the burned acreage into a memorial to his mother: RACHEL HUBE SPOONER PARK/ARGENTITE, COLORADO.

If the sentimental ending satirizes ancestor worship, William Peden, reviewing for the New York *Times*, still wondered if *Their Town*, after all, is not "a long joke in questionable taste."[7] To Cabot Cunningham, the one-sided developer Hube was an unsung hero, following in turn the armies of trappers, scouts, soldiers, and settlers—all making war on the West. To Peden, however, Hube Spooner is a symbol of "destructive American materialism," while Cunningham, involving himself in the Boer, Japanese-Russian, and Mexican Wars, is a "romantically damaged combination of Byron and Jefferson, a symbol of devotion to the cause of universal brotherhood."[8] *Saturday Review* saw Hube as "a Babbitt in softer focus than Sinclair Lewis' hero. . . ." Granting Steele's semisympathetic treatment, perhaps Hube Spooner is closer to a western version of Faulkner's Yoknapatawpha schemer, Flem Snopes. Of all the characters in *Their Town*, at any rate, only Hube is not wooden, although his muzzled-ox personality is monotonous.

Praising the novel as local history, Caroline Bancroft noted in her Denver *Post* review that *Their Town* is difficult to read;[9] but another potential partisan, H. G. Kincheloe of the Raleigh *News and Observer*, correctly listed the novel's faults: uncoordinated plot, theatrical style, and inept dialogue.[10] Indeed, words like "ticklement, muddlement, and startlement" we can consider as period slang, but we cannot excuse such skeins of clotty exegesis as the following:

Hube could not know, of course, that Kentucky's long-despaired-of pregnancy had come just in time to tie a restless Amy to Argentite again, however temporarily, and save the pair from what might well have been a breakup; for in those days it was Millard who cherished their and their growing daughter's home there, and the town. Nor, could Hube have realized it, would he have cared. He, who hadn't it in him to envy, was taken by its cousin, jealousy. His it was, not another's, to do the watching, the waiting-on, the tiptoeing about when Kentucky and the child in her womb napped. His, to cheer her when she drooped and pshaw it off as just the thing expected of her. His, not Amy's. (263)

Because *Their Town* lacks a sharp narrative line, its forceful scenes dissipate themselves in garrulous connections and in blocks of over- and underwritten prose.

X   The Way to the Gold

After *Their Town*, Steele fell seriously ill; the many years of seven-day weeks concluded in what he called "a good nervous bust-up."[11] During the post-World War II years, Doubleday published Steele at a steady loss; but following his recuperation, the editors, reviewing his talent, his early reputation, and his money-making *That Girl from Memphis*, contracted in the fall of 1953 for another book, Steele's last. Steele planned *The Last of the*

Robbers—his working title—as a sixty-thousand-word suspense novel about a contemporary search for one hundred thousand dollars cached in Washington State the generation before by the last of the great train robbers.

But during the 1953–54 winter on Florida's Sanibel Island, a rapidly aging Steele acceded to the manuscript's running itself to over ninety thousand words. In the summer of 1954, Doubleday found the simple story of the way to the gold almost obliterated by Steele's prolixity. A typescript of this original version among the Wilbur Daniel Steele Papers at Stanford University is indeed antithetical to the author's early devotion to (and capacity for) literary quintessence. With Steele's consent, Doubleday arranged with his agent, Harold Matson, to hire writer Evelyn Wells to work on the manuscript. Miss Wells deciphered Steele's "cunei-form," smoothed the style, played out the important scenes, and even suggested the inside-cover map of the route to the gold."[12] When the book finally appeared, Steele seemed fairly content.

If the plot of *The Way to the Gold* (1955) hinges on the con-temporary search for historical gold, the theme rests on the Amer-ican Dream. Before ex-reform schooler and "fall guy" Joe Mundy is pardoned from jail, his dying cellmate Ned Glazier (last of the train robbers) litanizes for him the complicated way to the gold. In the tradition of Steele's orphan-heroes, naïve Mundy dreams of wealth. Ever distrustful and friendless, he bumbles toward the cache. But in Greenbay, on northeastern Washington's Columbia River, he falls in love with Edith Clifford (a diner waitress called "Hank"); and he later finds himself the town hero when, Horatio Alger-like, he saves an influential family's dog. Besides Joe Mundy, others in Greenbay seek the gold—undercover agents and cagey descendants of the old robber gang. For their own ends, each befriends Joe and Hank, who wait for a chance to snatch the treasure.

Finally, on their rugged way to the gold, newlyweds Joe and Hank realize, independently, that all one truly desires is within (love) and without (friends). But soon after each penetrates the other's loyalty, shadowing agents and shadowing descendants emerge from the woods in a series of showdowns, until the forces of law and order prevail. In the end, a treasury agent, the "new" Joe and the "new" Hank mark the gold's location—under a slab covered by tons of mud at the botton of an enormous lake made when the Grand Coulee Dam backed up the Columbia River.

Although *The Way to the Gold* has a contemporary setting and, as a result of heavy editing, is more direct than Steele's earlier Western narratives, it sounds almost as old-fashioned. In spite of its desperadoes and its hidden loot, the novel, as Martin Levin pointed out in *Saturday Review*, "has an air of happy innocence that belongs to another day."[13] Indeed, the novel seems not only negatively harmless—without malice—but positively innocuous. Acknowledging its display of skillful plotting, feeling for character, and values in an acquisitive society, Herbert West in the New York *Times* ended by satirizing the tale for its heavy-handed, Norman Vincent Peale moral: "that true riches are where the heart is, that love, respect, and a feeling of belonging, even in a community as drab as Greenbay, are worth more than all the gold in Fort Knox."[14] Indeed, like *Their Town*, *The Way to the Gold* answers a resounding "Nothing" to the biblical "What shall it profit a man, if he shall gain the whole world, and lose his own soul?" But Joe Mundy's intensified moral consciousness at the end is laboriously trite.

Because of the last chapter, Steele's qualified contentment with the outside rewriting slowly waxed to anger; for he came to regard the book as "butchered to the point of meaninglessness."[15] In Steele's mind, the role of the treasury agent was diminished too much, as was the logic of loyalty between Joe and Hank. What angered him most, however, was the titillating emergence from the woods of the robbers' sadistic descendants. Originally, only four characters—Joe, Hank, the treasury agent, and the agent's old partner (deleted from the narrative)—were involved in the final search. To be sure, Steele's original ending is more honest and less melodramatic; but, ironically, the published novel, with its sensational ending and glib style aimed at the large popular audience, sold only around three thousand copies, a far cry from *That Girl from Memphis* (sixty-three thousand copies). The publishers now paid for the reaction against knotty *Diamond Wedding* (fourteen thousand copies) and *Their Town* (seven thousand copies).

XI *Gerontion*

Nonetheless, Twentieth-Century Fox bought the story, and with the proceeds Steele and Norma sold Seven Acres and built a small house nearby on Terry Road in Old Lyme on the Connecticut River. Then began for both him and Norma a variety of enervating hospitalizations and operations. In the summer of 1956, the weary writer wrote to his sister Muriel: "I am trying to learn again how to put words together and how to dream up a story worth the words. Maybe I'll make it, I don't know."[16] But by winter he wrote to his sister Beulah: "In the loss of the ability to create as a writer—to deal either with ideas or words—I presume I am in the company of a horde of others of my years, so I'd better learn to take it."[17]

Once a traveler and reveler, Steele at seventy-one regarded himself and his wife as near senile hermits, and the townspeople viewed them as village eccentrics. His Provincetown shyness returned, and he studiously avoided people, including the progression of students who came to inquire about "Footfalls" or "How Beautiful with Shoes." In 1958, Steele wrote to Muriel that he was setting himself "the chore of forgetting the shape and meaning of words."[18] Although he donated volumes of his stories and his inscribed O'Neill plays to the local library, he relied on the Alice Rogers Bookshop for the latest mysteries. A passage in a story Steele first published in 1931—"The Body of the Crime"—foreshadows this period of his life: "It was good for Daniel [Kinsman] he had the book called *Murder*! At the end of his emotional tether he must have escape, and the surest escape was here between these covers; he knew the taste of it beforehand, as the eater of drugs knows the taste of his drug. Escape, yes. And a curious, helpless, rather horrid surrender" (356).

Harried by Norma during their 1958–59 winter on Sanibel Island, Steele gave up playing dead; he responded to two assignments: a haunting commencement essay—"Out of Nothing—Something"—for Old Lyme High School and a powerful half-hour radio adaptation of his story "The Black Road"—retitled "It's a Million" —for Paul Green and the University of North Carolina. Back in Old Lyme, Steele, now a shut-in, wrote to Paul Green in the winter of 1959: "The precious, ecstatic agony of the words and sentences which went into the radio thing. Doing what I was certain I would never do again."[19]

During the 1960's Steele watched himself and Norma grow progressively senile. On June 13, 1960, Thurston committed suicide in Rhode Island. To add to life's burdens, Steele began losing more hearing and Norma more sight. Rereading some of his early novels during this period, he thought *Storm* best; *Meat*, good; and *Isles of the Blest*, fair. Occasionally Steele watched someone's adaptation of one of his dimly remembered stories on television, but he refused to see the film version of *The Way to the Gold.*[20] Needing special care by 1964, on April 13 the Steeles entered the Essex Rest Home, a few miles up river from Old Lyme. At first Steele, tall and bony, played the role of rest-home clown and wit; but after a few months, he became so depressed that he was transferred to a hospital for observation. On a piece of cardboard, he scrawled his last fragmentary message to the world: "Attention Attention Dear Friends—I am incarcerated at convalescent home. Here I have walked back and forth (between short sleeps, my knees buckling and my thoughts at home and. . . .)"[21]

On February 4, 1965, Steele and Norma were admitted to Highland Hall Convalescent Hospital in Essex, Connecticut. On May 29, 1967, Norma died; three years later—on May 26, 1970—Steele died. Both lie in Pleasant View Cemetery, not far from Seven Acres. During the last years of his long and productive life, Wilbur Daniel Steele spent most of his waking hours in the limbo of his sunny room, where he teased the shadow on his grizzled lip and stared into heaven.

CHAPTER 9

Conclusion

VIRTUALLY unknown by students today and ignored by critics, Wilbur Daniel Steele nevertheless is an important transitional figure in the history of the American short story. Students of the genre, perhaps too ready to classify writers as pejoratively "old" or "new," have not explained (or explained away) the fact that from the mid-1910's to the early 1930's readers and teachers sensitive to the demands of the short story regarded Steele as America's leading master of the form. Evidently, sympathizers for the "new" felt about him as did F. Scott Fitzgerald, who in 1938 advised a scholar against including the storyteller in a projected survey of contemporary literature: "Why Wilbur Daniel Steele, who left no mark whatever, invented nothing, created nothing except a habit of being an innocuous part of the O'Brien anthology?"[1] That Steele apparently had little influence on the direction of the "new story" does not mean that he neither invented nor created stories of literary merit and historical importance. To be sure, Steele's popularity, especially among the intelligent middle class, grew out of his own liberal but rigorously civilized formative years in Denver; but this fact in itself does not make for a pallid esthetic. Read singly or over, say, a dozen years, Steele's uniquely grim stories doubtlessly oppress much less than they do when one systematically moves through seven collections—or even through this critical-analytical study.

Until he relinquished his hold on the short story, Steele gave full validity neither to the internal nor to the external world. As more and more "formless" case history and social documentation shaped the "life-like" stories in the little and the cultural magazines, influential critics and intellectuals consumed by burning issues rising out of front-page social, political, and economic contexts tended to regard as irrelevant Steele's well-wrought, atmospheric "fourth acts" of private paradox and specific irony. After fifteen years of daily toil (ones which terminated in the death of his charming, talented first wife), Steele found his mental and emotional resources sapped, his great potential gone. In describing the hero of "Footfalls," Steele prefigured his own loss: "Nothing in his life had been so hard to meet as this insidious drain of distrust in his own powers; this sense of a traitor within the walls" (291). With the help of his vibrant and able second wife, Steele resigned himself to change by turning first to the theater and then to the novel. In both ventures commercial failure followed commercial success—without benefit of critical success.

Today, many view Steele's innermost conviction of *life as struggle* as hopelessly Naturalistic—and *struggle as Godly* as hopelessly Romantic. But, unlike Anderson, Wolfe, Hemingway, among many others, Steele only infrequently projected literal autobiography into his fiction: "I seem," he once wrote, "to be pretty much the common or garden variety of person. . . . My main desire is to have the moon."[2] Unable to oblige readers who demanded restricted Realism and personal confession, Steele preferred to reshape what he saw and felt into something—a pictorial precept—that tried to be profoundly true rather than shockingly factual. He well realized that ideas have opposites and that he might be "at least half wrong about things"—but those who thought otherwise "also were half wrong."[3]

Unesthetically instructive in his attenuated or sprawling novels, Steele in his stories is nearly always appropriately moral. Time and again, he dramatized the tough-minded thesis that *experience* teaches us that: "Virtue leads as checkered a career as Vice, that Reputability often goes about in strange garments, that Good and Evil are sometimes only the way the penny turns, and that Life is forever getting her heroes and villains mixed" (*Storm*, 113). Whether the fortunes of Steele's characters are good or bad, successful or unsuccessful, their outcomes grow from an unpredictable inevitability; and they usually stand in some heavy-handed ironic juxtaposition to their beginnings.

In comparing stories of the early 1920's with those of the early 1940's, Steele affirmed that vision is in the eyes, not in objects, and that roughly twenty years separates a writer's seeing from his telling. Steele wrote his own stories, he argued, out of a way of seeing the world of foreign concord and domestic activity at the turn of the century—when plot served the process of *doing* rather than of *feeling*, when stories exemplified pragmatic optimism: "U.S.A., of the Golden Age. . . . Life skipping pages in its eagerness to know, of anything, what came of it: the Happy Ending.

And the happy ending was no mere catchpenny escape mechanism of those days. It was solid realism. It was such matter-of-fact in the faith of then, that most men discover gold mines on grub-stakes and die wealthy, as it came to be in a later faith, that most men buy utilities on margin and live unhappily ever afterward."[4]

In the great Romantic tradition of Scott, Hawthorne, Stevenson, and Kipling, Steele tried to stir his readers' imaginations and to involve them in imaginary problems of individual morality by *heightening* empirical existence. Where a local-color Realist might do well to capture the literalness of, say, daily life in south Denver, the quasi-aristocratic, quasi-bohemian Anglo-Saxon from the Rockies ventured among the Portuguese of Cape Cod, the Negroes of the Caribbean, and the Semites of Algeria. Exotic novelty, though no more *externally* real than domestic familiarity, was for the incurable Romantic more real *internally*.

Educated contemporaries found in Steele not only escape from the everyday, but—more important—entrance into another place, another culture, another way of looking at life. Whether set at home or abroad, his stories embody a kind of unschematized history of certain values prevailing in America before and, to a lesser extent, following World War I. To such "Romantic" themes as suspected innocence, revenge and retribution, power of love or friendship, validity of premonition, and return from the "dead," Steele brought sinewy new twists; and through mystification he ironically clarified such "Realistic" ideas as heredity versus environment, law and conscience, divided self, quest for identity, and individual awakening. "Mystification is a good thing sometimes," Steele once wrote. "It gives the brain a fillip, stirs memory, puts the gears of imagination in mesh" ("Footfalls," 299).

Mimetically accurate—almost parodic—when necessary, Steele lured the reader from "normality" to an epistemological reality. In heightening the commonplace (Wordsworth's lyrical intent), Steele's "whole-cloth" mind also heightened coincidence to the point of "statistical" improbability—thus disturbing Aristotelians as well as champions of the "new" literary order. Apparently Steele's diplomatic silence contributed more to his desired effects (but less to his later reputation) than would even glancing references to hoary miracle or the hypothesis that events random to one set of laws might well be ordered to another. A world geared to expedient scientific determinism finds Steele's tacit but outmoded "chance" too "easy."

While transcending conventional stories, Steele did not abandon himself to the exhilarating freedom, even license, of the new informalism. Indeed, stories highly conscious, highly controlled, and highly unified are not incompatible with high art—even though older harmonies inevitably give way to newer ones. A master of Classical plot on the order of Sophoclean symmetry and a brilliant exploiter of inherent linguistic consecutiveness, Steele (like Poe) subordinated parts to the whole. Thus readers seeking a chain of "dramatic moments" sometimes find Steele's melodramas tedious.

Trained morally and esthetically to deplore loose ends, Steele perhaps too militantly forced chaos into order. In "Eternal Youth" he made a passing reference to the common ground of secular predestination and artistic design: "the last note strikes the key for the whole piece and pulls it together into something."[5] Steele's long search for ironic unities coincided, of course, with the kind of literary ending made fashionable by O. Henry's generation. Steele's analytical frame of mind and detective imagination (focused as it was on individual predicament and metaphysical puzzle—*"Who am I? What is happening?"*) were eminently suited to problem-solving. Where Sherwood Anderson, in turn, achieved effect by simply raising problems, many young writers now achieve effect by dramatizing the difficulty or the impossibility of even doing so.

Today the device of literary problem-solving engenders nearly as much mirthful groaning as a non-Joycean pun. But far less meretricious than O. Henry's proverbial endings, Steele's "twists" generally offer a profounder response to dilemma. Momentarily, at least, the sense of completion liberates us from time and space. Through authoritative indirection and bold inference, Steele stages in silent print the eternal drama between appearance and reality. Formal surprise forces us to see what we missed seeing the first time.

To his literary formalism and to his psychological Romance Steele brought his early training in art. Unable to abide Hollywood, he early foresaw the possibilities in the film for combining pictorial with narrative art. His idiosyncratic application of "picture" to "word" is obvious. Like the Impressionists, Steele achieved his effects through suggestion. Like Corot, he favored *plein* settings: landscapes, seascapes, village streets, and figure studies. (Even sedentary Henry James saw Cape Cod as a delightful little triumph of Impressionism.) Like Courbet, Steele heightened "common" subjects. Like Morisot's brushwork, Steele's style is dense yet subtle. Like Manet's vignettes, Steele's scenes are bold. So conscious of

impression was Steele that, as a young writer, he summoned up
Stephen Crane's celebrated line in *The Red Badge of Courage*
("The sun was pasted in the sky like a red wafer") and reworked
it in *Storm* to the point of parody: "The sun reclined on the sky-
line like a florid, rotten melon" (71).

When not eclipsed by formalism or by Impressionism, Steele's
characters seem beautifully wedded to the baroque language of
the whole story. The outcome of a character caught in the grip
of circumstance is sometimes determined more by the quality of
his soul than by the quality of his environment—enough to provide
some readers with the sensation of antiquarianism. Usually, Steele's
central character is a hero, heroine, villain, or vixen out of Romanticism curiously combined with an ambiguous victim, antihero or
antiheroine, out of Realism. Steele's dramatis personae is wide,
ranging from sophisticates who speak the "King's English" (or
some other language), to the general American, to an assortment
of primitives who speak the local patois. His onomatopoeically
named individuals with their emblematic furniture curiously suggest such universal types as fatal female, pastoral innocent, hypocritical moralist, naïve minister, prodigal son, and revengeful husband. Even Steele's psychotics hover somewhere between the
madman of Romance and the sick creature of Realism.

By boldly manipulating point of view and time, Steele created
rare effects. As in Erckmann-Chatrian and in Conrad, many melodramatic actions in Steele cling to the point of view of the speaker,
who may or may not be an eyewitness. This device contributes to
Steele's double effect of illusion and reality. Simultaneously filter-
ing reality and gaining esthetic distance, cross-sectioning incidents,
shuttling back and forth in displaced time, Steele's first-person narrator is himself part of the story's total meaning. Although the narrator has no control over what is *happening*, his understanding of
what finally has *happened* is a kind of Kantian construction on the
chaos of the external world. What appears to be an almost Naturalistic objectivity serves to counterpoint the hysteria in the story
proper. But even Steele's brand of hysteria seems a little outdated.

Since the end of World War II, only a few critics have com-
mented about Steele. On the one hand, Ray West notes no "vigorous social attitudes"—only "brilliant surface glitter."[6] On the
other hand, George K. Anderson sees "both beauty and cruelty . . .
as well as a strangeness which is not freakish, a disquieting mood
which is not merely shocking—and always an originality which
expresses itself with firmness and courage."[7] In their *Great Ameri-*

can Short Stories, Wallace and Mary Stegner view Steele as a syn-thesis of James' "psychological curiosity," Crane's "bright impres-sionism," and the local colorists' "careful sense of place."[8] And the mother in Violet Weingarten's disturbing *Atlantic Monthly* story of 1966, entitled "The Man Who Saw Through Heaven," muses that America's youth has found none of that "triumphant" feeling of the hero of Steele's masterpiece.[9]

In spite of Poe's no doubt biased assertion that in prose the short story affords the fairest field for the exercise of the loftiest talent, literary history still discriminates against the "mere" story writer. To judge a "professional" writer like Steele, who gained a distinguished reputation from his bread-and-butter stories (but nothing *but* bread and butter from his plays and novels), requires an imaginative extension tantamount to a moral exercise. If our plethora of distinguished younger writers is excluded, a list of America's finest short-story writers might include Washington Irving, Edgar Allan Poe, Nathaniel Hawthorne, Bret Harte, Sarah Orne Jewett, Stephen Crane, Henry James, O. Henry, Sherwood Anderson, Ring Lardner, William Saroyan, Ernest Hemingway, William Faulkner, Katherine Anne Porter, and Eudora Welty. If in his greatest work—*The Best Stories of Wilbur Daniel Steele* (1945)—Steele brought to and gave to the form of the short story less than some of those listed brought and gave—less creative imagination and invention, less purity of concentration, less ra-tional control, less emotional response to life, a lower pitch of in-telligence, and fewer linguistic resources—I fail to detect it.

Today Steele appears old-fashioned and reactionary, not be-cause he lacks fantastic literary skill, but because fictional state-ments now in vogue are so different. Steele's imaginative realities and linguistic structures are made from words and from literary patterns that are not part of our current empirical reality. But, like Stevenson, O. Henry, and Kipling, Steele deserves to be "re-discovered"—if not in our time, then in another. If discriminating anthologists continue to reprint Steele's classic efforts, that time is sure to come. But if anthologists submit to the tyranny of the moment, then even John Updike and Bernard Malamud are in jeopardy.

The accolade once given to a fine story—to a Steele story—was "How extraordinary!" Then the accolade became "How true!" Writing for the Twenty-fifth Anniversary Edition of the 1943 *O. Henry Prize Stories,* Wilbur Daniel Steele recognized that, be-yond question, the laudatory response "How true!" has made for a deeper, wider, more mature, more abundant literature. He added: "Just as it is beyond question that no story was, nor ever can be, truly extraordinary, without first and foremost being true."[10]

Notes and References

Chapter One

1. Founded in 1873 by the Freedmen's Aid Society of the Methodist Episcopal Church in the basement of a Negro Methodist church in Greensboro, the college originally was coeducational. Today Bennett is a four-year liberal arts college for women, most of them blacks. Wilbur F. Steele Hall (1922), now the fine-arts building, stands opposite the Student Union.

2. Winnifred King Rugg, "Wilbur Daniel Steele" (typescript at Denver Public Library), p. 10. Also, the jacket of *The Best Stories of Wilbur Daniel Steele* (New York, 1945) states: "I probably owe more than any other story writer to O. Henry."

3. Wilbur Fletcher Steele, letter to Blanche Colton Williams, July 1, 1920.

4. *Who Was Who, 1897-1942*, p. 1174. Reverend Steele's other books: *Commentary on Joshua* (1873), *Love Enthroned* (1875), *The Milestone Papers* (1878), *Commentary on Leviticus and Numbers* (1891), *Half Hours with St. Paul* (1895), *The Defense of Christian Perfection* (1896), *Gospel of the Comforter* (1897), *Jesus Exultant* (1899), *A Substitute for Holiness* (1899), *Half Hours with St. John's Epistles* (1901), and *Steele's Answers* (1912).

5. Charles J. F. Binney, *Genealogy of the Binney Family* (Albany, 1886), pp. 98-99.

6. Wilbur Fletcher Steele, letter to Blanche Colton Williams, July 1, 1920.

7. Perhaps Steele's first story — an unfinished bit of fantasy written when he was fourteen — is entitled "A Trip to Jupiter, 1970." Full of astronomical detail, it begins: "When I was young some friends and I chartered an air ship for a summer trip in the solar system."

8. William Fletcher Steele, letter to Blanche Colton Williams, July 1, 1920.

9. *Tower of Sand* (New York and London, 1929), p. 181.

10. Wilbur Fletcher Steele, letter to Blanche Colton Williams, July 1, 1920. In a letter to his father, January 24, 1931, Wilbur Daniel Steele wrote: "I love you so much, and admire you, as I always have, more than any other person in the world. You have given me so much,

I hope I shan't squander it. Perhaps what you've given me of spirit and character is precisely what will keep me from squandering it."

11. *The Man Who Saw Through Heaven* (New York and London, 1927), p. 67.

12. Steele's brother Arthur died at Saint Luke's Hospital, Denver, April 17, 1897.

13. *Tower of Sand*, pp. 181-82.

14. Wilbur Fletcher Steele, letter to Blanche Colton Williams, July 1, 1920.

15. *Kynewisbok* (Denver, 1907), pp. 212, 214, 225, 240.

16. Letter to family, December 18, 1907.

17. Dilly Tante, ed., *Living Authors* (New York, 1931), p. 382.

18. Letter to family, 1908.

19. Interview with Peter Steele, June 30, 1966.

20. Tante, p. 382.

21. *Storm* (New York, 1914), p. 31.

22. Letter to family, October 2, 1909.

23. "The Islanders," *Harper's Magazine*, CXXVII (July, 1913), 273.

24. Letter to family, October 24, 1909. Steele's roommates were Howard Brubaker, an editor of *Success Magazine*; Earl Needham, a political muckraker; and Paul Wilson, in the Bureau of Municipal Research.

25. Letter to sister Beulah, January 6, 1910.

26. Letter to mother, November 25, 1909.

27. *Urkey Island* (New York, 1926), p. 211.

28. Letter to family, April 12, 1910.

29. Letter to family, February 5, 1911.

30. Letter to family, June 12, 1911. For an account of the legend, see Mary Heaton Vorse, *Time and the Town* (New York, 1942), pp. 193-94.

31. Letter to family, March 12, 1912.

32. On February 17, 1913, in Brookline, Massachusetts, Steele married Margaret Orinda Thurston, daughter of Dr. Rufus L. Thurston's widow.

33. Clara E. Fanning, ed., *Book Review Digest:1914* (New York, 1915), p. 504.

34. "Mr. Steele's Story of Cape Cod Life," New York *Times Book Review*, March 22, 1914, p. 133.

35. In a letter to his family, November 7, 1914, Steele claims that he borrowed the name "Pa Jim" from an actual fisherman. Also, Manta's father and mother resemble Steele's friends, the Avellars. Old Harbor's Peaked Hill, Snail Road, and Wood End appear on maps, but Back Water is a "highly fictitious region known as Great Neck Island—seven knots N.N.E. of nowhere."

36. Letter to family, October 18, 1914.

37. Letter to family, March 22, 1915.

38. Letter to family, February 18, 1915.

39. Vorse, *Time and the Town*, p. 122.

40. Susan Glaspell, *"The Road to the Temple"* (New York, 1927), p. 251.

41. Helen Deutsch and Stella Hanau, *The Provincetown* (New York, 1931), p. 14.

42. *Isles of the Blest* (New York, 1924), pp. 78-79.

43. "At the Ocean Cross-Roads," *Harper's Magazine*, CXXXV (October, 1917), 688.

44. *Ibid.*, 689.

45. *Ibid.*

46. *Ibid.*, 692.

47. "Beleaguered Island," *Harper's Magazine*, CXXXVI (May, 1918), 819.

48. Edward J. O'Brien, letter to Steele, December 14, 1917.

49. O'Brien, ed., *Best Short Stories of 1915* (New York, 1916), p. vi.

50. O'Brien, ed., *Best Short Stories of 1916*, p. iv.

51. O'Brien, ed., *Best Short Stories of 1917*, p. xvii.

52. Theodore Peterson, *Magazines in the Twentieth Century* (Urbana, 1964), p. 410.

53. O'Brien, "The Best Sixty-Three American Short Stories of 1917," *Bookman*, XLVI (February, 1918), 706.

54. Letter to family, October 27, 1918.

Chapter Two

1. "Latest Works of Fiction," New York *Times Book Review*, September 15, 1918, p. 387.

2. "Notes on New Books," The *Dial*, LXV (October, 1918), 274.

3. Letter to family, February 28, 1920.

4. Henry Goodman, ed., *Creating the Short Story* (New York, 1929), p. 135.

5. Letter to family, January 16, 1910.

6. Letter to sister Muriel, February 2, 1919.

7. Letter to sister Beulah, August 2, 1919.

8. Letter to sister Muriel, May 12, 1919. Muriel Steele's "Mr. Blue, Kidnapper," *Harper's Magazine*, CXXXIX (July, 1919), 264-76, is a spritely Mr. Wrennian comedy.

9. *The Man Who Saw Through Heaven*, p. 319.

10. Wilbur Fletcher Steele, letter to Blanche Colton Williams, July 1, 1920.

11. *The Shame Dance* (New York, 1923), p. 348.

12. Archibald Henderson, Raleigh *News and Observer*, May 16, 1928.

13. Harvey Breit, "Talk with Mr. Steele," New York *Times Book Review,* August 6, 1950, p. 12.

14. *Urkey Island,* p. 42.

15. Rugg, *op. cit.*

16. *Ibid.*

17. Letters to family, December 12, 1929; March 8, 1922.

18. "Commuters in Barbary," *Harper's Magazine,* CXLIII (July, 1921), 147.

19. "In the Mountains of the Desert," *Harper's Magazine,* CXLIII (November, 1921), 784.

20. Letter to family, December 5, 1922.

Chapter Three

1. T. H. D., "Books," *Boston Transcript,* June 9, 1923, p. 4.

2. C. M. Puckette, *Literary Review* (June, 1923), 783.

3. D. K. Laub, "Book Reviews," Detroit *News,* October 7, 1923, p. 19.

4. Marion A. Knight and Mertice M. James, eds., *Book Review Digest:1923* (New York, 1924), p. 491.

5. "Latest Works of Fiction," New York *Times Book Review,* June 10, 1923, pp. 17-18.

6. Blanche Colton Williams, ed., *O. Henry Memorial Prize Stories of 1921,* p. xvi.

7. Letter to family, December 30, 1921.

8. "New Books in Brief," *The Independent,* CXIV (January 24, 1925), 106.

9. A tepid drunken-drowning version of Hepar's suicide appeared also in *Pictorial Review* (November, 1923) under the title "Ginger Beer."

10. Letter to family, November 13, 1924.

11. Henry Seidel Canby, *Saturday Review of Literature,* I (April 25, 1925), 712.

12. Steele dedicated the book to his mother, "one of those dear and 'terrible' women who know where things are . . ."; also, Martha Hume reacts to her son's barking much as Steele's mother reacted.

13. John Farrar, "Taboo," *Bookman,* LXII (September, 1925), 74.

14. Knight and Jones, eds., *Book Review Digest: 1925* (New York, 1926), p. 671.

15. Lloyd Morris, *Saturday Review of Literature,* II (December 5, 1925), 362-63.

16. Louis Bromfield, New York *Herald Tribune,* September 20, 1925, p. 5.

17. Van Vechten Hostetter, New York *World,* September 6, 1925, p. 4m.

18. Letter to family, October 3, 1925.

19. Judges for the *Harper's* Award were Meredith Nicholson, Bliss Perry, and Zona Gale. Julian Street received the first-prize money in the O. Henry competition for "Mr. Bisbee's Princess."

20. Letter to family, August 14, 1926.

21. Frank Elser, *Bookman*, LXX (February, 1927), 691.

22. Letter to family, October 12, 1926.

Chapter Four

1. "New Books in Brief," *The Independent*, CXVI (April 24, 1926), 498.

2. Allan Nevins, *Saturday Review of Literature*, II (May 29, 1926), 822.

3. *The Best Stories of Wilbur Daniel Steele* (New York, 1945), p. 333.

4. Lewis H. Chrisman, *Literary Digest*, IV (July, 1926), 527.

Chapter Five

1. "Mr. Steele's Stories," New York *Times Book Review*, November 6, 1927, p. 7.

2. Clifton Fadiman, *Nation*, CXXV (December 28, 1927), 738.

3. *Ibid.*

4. "Drama," New York *Herald Tribune*, July 25, 1950, p. 3.

5. Blanche Colton Williams, ed., *Short Stories for College Classes* (New York, 1930), p. 419.

6. Letter to family, October 3, 1930.

7. Jane Wyman played the lead in Alvin Sapinsley's television adaptation of "When Hell Froze" for Chrysler Theater, February 2, 1966.

8. Max Wylie, letter to Martin Bucco, February 24, 1966. Wylie's adaptation was performed on November 10, 1938. Douglas Coulter, *Columbia Workshop Plays* (New York, 1939), pp. 181-214, describes the adaptation as capturing Steele's "loneliness and terror and moral disintegration."

9. Letter to family, November 10, 1927.

10. Rugg, *op. cit.*, p. 10.

11. *Ibid.*

12. Gladys Graham, *Saturday Review of Literature*, IV (March 10, 1928), 666.

13. Letter to family, n.d. [1929].

Chapter Six

1. Edwin Seaver, New York *Evening Post*, November 9, 1929, p.

11m. Also unaware of the original publication dates, the reviewer for the New York *Times,* December 8, 1929, p. 9, asserted that Steele was becoming more expert in handling his "treacherous tools—irony, symbolism, and plot development."

2. Paul Allen, *Bookman,* LXX (December, 1929), 448. Photograph portrait of Steele by Doris Ulmann, p. 431.

3. M. C. Dawson, New York *Herald Tribune,* January 5, 1930, p. 10.

4. Williams, ed., *O. Henry Prize Stories of 1919,* p. xxii.

5. Beulah Jenness, letter to Martin Bucco, July 10, 1966.

6. Letter to family, December 12, 1919.

7. Letter to family, January 25, 1929.

8. Letter to family, February 7, 1930.

9. Committee of North Carolina English Teachers, eds., *North Carolina Authors* (Chapel Hill, 1952), p. 116.

10. "Ropes" originally sold to Fox Films in 1921 for $2500. *Undertow* was copyrighted in 1930 by Universal Pictures Corporation. The novelette, published by Jacobsen (New York, 1930), was based on the motion-picture version.

11. "Dedication of Steele Hall," Greensboro *Daily News,* November 5, 1930, p. 12.

12. Interview with Paul Green, July 17, 1966. Homan Macy of "Man and Boy" is modeled, in part, on Green.

13. Letter to sister Beulah, January 4, 1931.

14. Letter to Paul Green, October 8, 1931.

15. Letter to Paul Green, November 25, 1931.

16. Daughter of a mining engineer, Norma grew up in Brookline, as did Margaret Steele. After a weary round of fashionable schools, Norma exhibited theatrical rather than social aspirations. To her parents' dismay, she went from John Craig's Boston Stock Company to New York, Australia, and England, appearing as an ingenue in *Her Husband's Wife.* Later she wrote one-act skits, including *Her Morning Bath,* part of the *Ritz Review,* and appeared with Helen Hayes in *To the Ladies* and with Marjorie Rambeau in *Why Not?* She had the lead in *Dancing Mothers.* Her comedy *Cradle Snatchers* (written with Russell Medcraft) opened at the Music Box Theatre, New York, in 1925 and ran for 478 performances. Later it was made into the musical *Let's Face It.*

17. Letter to sister Muriel, January 19, 1933.

18. Letter to sister Beulah, February 13, 1935.

19. Brooks Atkinson, New York *Times,* December 5, 1934, p. 28.

20. "New Plays," *Time,* XXVI (December 9, 1935), 54.

21. Gilbert Gabriel, *Literary Digest,* CXX (December 14, 1935), 19.

22. Letter to sister Beulah, January 11, 1936.

23. "Mysteries of the Month," *Time,* XXXI (March, 1938), 64.

24. Among Steele's unpublished, unproduced plays at Stanford University are: *Any Woman, Diamond Wedding, Dragon's Teeth, John Addam, This Day Between,* and *When Hell Froze*—all three-act plays, several of them written in collaboration with Norma.

25. Letter to sister Beulah, February, 1943.

26. Letter to Paul and Elizabeth Green, February, 1943.

27. Denver *Post,* clipping, n.d., Denver Public Library.

28. Gay Wilson Allen, New York *Times Book Review,* June 10, 1945, p. 5.

29. *Ibid.,* p. 36.

30. Letter to sister Beulah, May 27, 1949.

Chapter Seven

1. Orville Prescott, *Yale Review,* XXXVI (Autumn, 1946), 192.

2. *Ibid.*

3. Edith Mirrielees, New York *Times Book Review,* July 14, 1946, p. 20.

4. For a recent survey of stories in this popular genre, see William Peden's "Sick in Mind and Body Both," *The American Short Story: Front Line in the National Defense of Literature* (Boston, 1964), pp. 87-131.

5. DeLancey Ferguson, *Weekly Book Review,* July 28, 1946, p. 5.

6. Dale L. Morgan, *Saturday Review of Literature,* XXXIII (August 5, 1950), 15.

7. Walter Van Tilburg Clark, New York *Times Book Review,* July 23, 1950, p. 4.

8. "Diamond Wedding," *Woman's Home Companion,* LVII (September, 1930), 17-19.

Chapter Eight

1. Mary Ross, New York *Herald Tribune,* December 9, 1951, p. 8.

2. John Brooks, New York *Times Book Review,* December 16, 1951, p. 16.

3. "Reactionary Old Fogy," *Time,* LVIII (December 10, 1951), 116.

4. Clark Kinnaird, New York *Journal-American,* December 22, 1951, p. 8.

5. "Reactionary Old Fogy," *Time,* p. 116.

6. R. H. Dillon, *Library Journal,* LXXVII (August, 1952), 1303.

7. William Peden, New York *Times Book Review,* August 10, 1952, p. 6.

8. *Ibid.*

9. Caroline Bancroft, Denver *Post,* August 10, 1952, p. 6E.

10. H. G. Kincheloe, Raleigh *News and Observer*, August 10, 1952, n.p.

11. Letter to sister Muriel, January 6, 1953.

12. Lee Barker, letter to Evelyn Wells, January 31, 1955.

13. Martin Leven, *Saturday Review of Literature*, XXXVIII (August 27, 1955), 12.

14. Herbert F. West, New York *Times*, July 31, 1955, p. 4.

15. Letter to sister Beulah, July 24, 1955.

16. Letter to sister Muriel, May 9, 1956.

17. Letter to sister Beulah, January 2, 1957.

18. Letter to sister Muriel, February 12, 19[58]. Rarely "lit'ry" in his fiction. Steele alludes in his letters mostly to Stevenson, Kipling, Carlyle, W. W. Jacobs, Barrie, Poe, Balzac, and Browning.

19. Letter to Paul Green, February 20, 1959.

20. *The Way to the Gold*, Twentieth Century-Fox, starring Jeffrey Hunter, Neville Brand, and Sheree North.

21. Letter to Joseph and Margaret Spada.

Chapter Nine

1. F. Scott Fitzgerald,, letter to Dayton Kohler, March 4, 1938. Andrew Turnbull, ed., *The Letters of F. Scott Fitzgerald* (New York, 1963), p. 571.

2. Stanley Kunitz and Howard Haycroft, eds., *Twentieth Century Authors* (New York, 1942), p. 1333.

3. Letter to sister Beulah, February 3, 1927.

4. Herschel Brickell, ed., *O. Henry Memorial Prize Stories of 1943*, p. xxii.

5. "Eternal Youth," *Scribner's Magazine*, LXIII (April, 1918), 482.

6. Ray B. West, *The Short Story in America* (Chicago, 1956), p. 81.

7. George K. Anderson and Eda Lou Walton, *This Generation* (Chicago, 1949), p. 668.

8. Wallace and Mary Stegner, *Great American Short Stories* (New York, 1957), p. 22.

9. Violet Weingarten, "The Man Who Saw Through Heaven," *Atlantic Monthly*, CCXVIII (September, 1966), 105.

10. Brickell, ed., *O. Henry Memorial Prize Stories of 1943*, p. xxiii.

Selected Bibliography

PRIMARY SOURCES

The Wilbur Daniel Steele Papers (approximately six hundred items) are housed at Stanford University Library. The collection includes manuscripts, correspondence, and numerous clippings. Steele-ana—both Wilbur Daniel and Wilbur Fletcher—also is in the University of Denver Archives.

A. Story Collections

Land's End and Other Stories. New York: Harper & Brothers, 1918.
The Shame Dance and Other Stories. New York: Harper & Brothers, 1923.
Urkey Island. New York: Harcourt, Brace, 1926.
The Man Who Saw Through Heaven and Other Stories. New York: Harper & Brothers, 1927.
Tower of Sand and Other Stories. New York: Harper & Brothers, 1929.
The Best Stories of Wilbur Daniel Steele. Garden City, N.Y.: Doubleday, Doran, 1945.
Full Cargo: More Stories. Garden City, N.Y.: Doubleday, Doran, 1951.

B. Plays

The Giant's Stair. New York: Appleton, 1924.
The Terrible Woman and Other One Act Plays. New York: Appleton, 1925.
Post Road. New York: Samuel French, 1935.

C. Novels

Storm. New York: Harper & Brothers, 1914.
Isles of the Blest. New York: Harper & Brothers, 1924.
Taboo. New York: Harcourt, Brace, 1925.
Meat. New York: Harper & Brothers, 1928.
Undertow. New York: Jacobsen, 1930.
Sound of Rowlocks. New York: Harper & Brothers, 1938.

That Girl from Memphis. Garden City, N.Y.: Doubleday, Doran, 1945.
Diamond Wedding. Garden City, N.Y.: Doubleday, Doran, 1950.
Their Town. Garden City, N.Y.: Doubleday, Doran, 1952.
The Way to the Gold. Garden City, N.Y.: Doubleday, Doran, 1955.

D. Selected Stories (°indicates collected story)

"On the Ebb Tide," *Success Magazine*, XIII (June, 1910), 339-401.
"Gloomy on the Gridiron," *Success Magazine*, XIII (November, 1910), 739-63.
"The Insurrecto," *National Magazine* (May, 1911), pp. 29-40.
"The Admirable Admirals," *Success Magazine*, XIV (October, 1911), 27-46.
°"White Horse Winter," *Atlantic Monthly*, CIX (April, 1912), 468-77.
"Thumbs Down," *Harper's Weekly*, LVI (August 3, 1912), 16-17.
"An Officer Born," *American Magazine*, LXXV (May, 1913), 24-28.
"The Islanders," *Harper's Magazine*, CXXVII (July, 1913), 268-73.
"The Handkerchief Lady's Girl," *Harper's Magazine*, CXXVIII (February, 1914), 463-71.
"Captain Ulysses G. Dadd, Retired," *Scribner's Magazine*, LVI (July, 1914), 117-28.
"The Wickedness of Father Veiera," *Atlantic Monthly*, CXIV (July, 1914), 59-69.
"The Younger Twin," *Harper's Magazine*, CXXIX (August, 1914), 464-72.
"Pa-Jim," *Scribner's Magazine*, LVI (November, 1914), 627-37.
"The Miracle," *The Masses*, VI (January, 1915), 5-6.
°"The Yellow Cat," *Harper's Magazine*, CXXX (March, 1915), 540-49.
"On Moon Hill," *Century Magazine*, XV (April, 1915), 2-13.
"A Matter of Education," *Harper's Magazine*, CXXXXI (May, 1915), 894-900.
"The Real Thing," *Century Magazine*, XC (May, 1915), 2-13.
°" 'Romance,' " *Atlantic Monthly*, CVX (June, 1915), 298-309.
"Free Agent," *Collier's Weekly*, LV (July 17, 1915), 5-6.
"Heritage," *Harper's Magazine*, CXXXI (July, 1915), 298-309.
°"The Killer's Son," *Harper's Magazine*, CXXXII (January, 1916), 199-209.
"Before the Mast," *Harper's Magazine*, CXXXII (March, 1916), 625-33.
°"Land's End," *Collier's Weekly*, LVII (March 25, 1916), 18-20.
°"Down on Their Knees," *Harper's Magazine*, CXXXIII (July, 1916), 213-24.
"The Last Fletcher," *Good Housekeeping*, LXIII (September, 1916), 35-37.

"An Escape from Freedom," *Harper's Magazine*, CXXXIII (October, 1916), 739-48.

*"A Devil of a Fellow," *Seven Arts*, I (November, 1916), 558-75.

*"White Hands," *Pictorial Review*, XVIII (January, 1917), 20-54.

"The Killers of Provincetown," *Harper's Magazine*, CXXXIV (March, 1917), 457-66.

"Mr. Timmons Tackles Life," *Harper's Magazine*, CXXXIV (April, May, 1917), 620-35, 849-62; CXXXV (June, 1917), 126-37.

*"Ching, Ching, Chinaman," *Pictorial Review*, XVIII (June, 1917), 5-28.

"The Half Ghost," *Harper's Magazine*, CXXXV (July, 1917), 241-50.

"Free," *Century Magazine*, XCIV (August, 1917), 518-26.

*"Ked's Hand," *Harper's Magazine*, CXXXV (September, 1917), 528-36.

"A Point of Honor," *Harper's Magazine*, CXXXV (November, 1917), 848-55.

*"The Woman at Seven Brothers," *Harper's Magazine*, CXXXV (December, 1917), 101-10.

*"The White Man," *Harper's Magazine*, CXXXVI (February, 1918), 423-31.

"You're Right, at That," *Collier's Weekly*, LX (February 23, 1918), 16-34.

*"The Wages of Sin," *Pictorial Review*, XIX (March, 1918), 8-10.

*"Always Summer," *Harper's Magazine*, CXXXVI (April, 1918), 692-700.

"Eternal Youth," *Scribner's Magazine*, LXIII (April, 1918), 473-83.

*"The Dark Hour," *Atlantic Monthly*, CXXI (May, 1918), 677-82.

*"A Man's a Fool," *Metropolitan*, XLVIII (June, 1918), 25-58.

"Mr. Scattergood and the Other World," *Harper's Magazine*, CXXXVII (July, 1918), 258-69.

"The Perfect Face," *Harper's Magazine*, CXXXVII (August, 1918), 362-68.

"A Taste of the Old Boy," *Collier's Weekly*, LXII (September 28, 1918), 11-25.

*"For Where Is Your Fortune Now?" *Pictorial Review*, XX (November, 1918), 27-35.

"The Heart of a Woman," *Harper's Magazine*, CXXXVIII (February, 1919), 384-91.

"Goodfellow," *Harper's Magazine*, CXXXVIII (April, 1919), 655-66.

*"For They Know Not What They Do," *Pictorial Review*, XX (July, 1919), 18-19.

"Accomplice After the Fact," *Good Housekeeping*, LXIX (August, 1919), 22-25.

*"Luck," *Harper's Magazine*, CXXXIX (August, 1919), 371-81.

*"La Guiablesse," *Harper's Magazine*, CXXXIX (September, 1919), 547-62.

"Clay and Cloven Hoof," *Harper's Magazine,* CXXXIX (October–November, 1919), 683-99, 889-906.

°"Out of Exile," *Pictorial Review,* XXI (November, 1919), 14-47.

°"Both Judge and Jury," *Harper's Magazine,* CXL (January, 1910), 179-88.

"God's Mercy," *Pictorial Review,* XXX (July–August, 1920), 17-88.

°"At Two-in-the-Bush," *Harper's Magazine,* CXL (October, 1920), 574-85.

°"Footfalls," *Pictorial Review,* XXII (October, 1920), 20-183.

°"The Shame Dance," *Harper's Magazine,* CXLII (December, 1920), 39-52.

"Fouled Anchor," *Harper's Magazine,* CXLII (April, 1921), 591-602.

" 'Toinette of Maisonnoir," *Pictorial Review,* XX (July, 1921), 13-44.

°"A Life," *Pictorial Review,* XXII (August, 1921), 5-72.

°"The Marriage in Kairwan," *Harper's Magazine,* CXLIV (December, 1921), 16-26.

°" 'He That Hideth His Secret,' " *Harper's Magazine,* CXLIV (February, 1922), 281-95.

°"The Mad," *Pictorial Review,* XXIII (July, 1922), 14-58.

°"From the Other Side of the South," *Pictorial Review,* XXIII (August, 1922), 12-49.

°"The Anglo-Saxon," *Harper's Magazine,* CXLV (August, 1922), 316-28.

°"The Man Who Sat," *Pictorial Review,* XXIII (September, 1922), 6-56.

"The First Born," *Pictorial Review,* XXIV (December, 1922), 14-42.

°" 'Arab Stuff,' " *Harper's Magazine,* CXLVI (January, 1923), 171-81.

°"Crocuses," *Pictorial Review,* XXIV (May, 1923), 8-34.

°"Tower of Sand," *Pictorial Review,* XIV (June, 1923), 5-30.

"Ginger Beer," *Pictorial Review,* XXV (November, 1923), 10-132.

°"What Do You Mean—Americans?," *Pictorial Review,* XXV (April, 1924), 8-9.

°" 'Lost at Sea,' " *Pictorial Review,* XXV (May, 1924), 5-7.

"Marriage," *Pictorial Review,* XXV (August, 1924), 12-13.

°"The Thinker," *Pictorial Review,* XXVI (December, 1924), 16-18.

"Sauce for the Goose," *Pictorial Review,* XXVI (January, 1925), 12-13.

°"Six Dollars," *Pictorial Review,* XXVI (March, 1925), 12-13.

°"When Hell Froze," *Harper's Magazine,* CL (May, 1925), 658-74.

°"The Man Who Saw Through Heaven," *Harper's Magazine,* CLI (September, 1925), 428-38.

°"Blue Murder," *Harper's Magazine,* CLI (October, 1925), 559-70.

°"Out of the Wind," *Pictorial Review,* XXVII (October, 1925), 11-13.

°"Brother's Keeper," *Harper's Magazine,* CLII (December, 1925), 78-83.

"Beauty," *Good Housekeeping,* LXXXII (January, 1926), 14-17.
*"The Gray Goose," *Harper's Magazine,* CLII (March, 1926), 411-23.
"Now I Lay Me," *Pictorial Review,* XXVII (April, 1926), 10-11.
*"Bubbles," *Harper's Magazine,* CLIII (August, 1926), 273-85.
*"Fe-Fi-Fo-Fum," *Pictorial Review,* XXVII (August, 1926), 14-16.
*"Autumn Bloom," *Pictorial Review,* XXVIII (November, 1926), 12-13.
*"A Drink of Water," *Harper's Magazine,* CLIV (January, 1927), 158-67.
*"Sailor! Sailor!," *Pictorial Review,* XXVII (July, 1927), 10-11.
"New Deal," *Scribner's Magazine,* LXXXII (August, 1927), 138-47.
*"Sooth," *Harper's Magazine,* CLV (August, 1927), 273-84.
"Speed," *Pictorial Review,* XXVIII (August, 1927), 14-15.
*"An American Comedy," *Pictorial Review,* XXIX (October, 1927), 9-85.
*"Mary Drake and Will Todd," *Pictorial Review,* XXIX (March–April, 1928), 11-23.
"Lightning," *Pictorial Review,* XXIX (June, 1928), 23-24.
*"Never Anything That Fades," *Harper's Magazine,* CLVII (June, 1928), 11-19.
"Satan Am a Snake," *Harper's Magazine,* CLVII (August, 1928), 304-13.
"Winter Wheat," *Pictorial Review,* XXIX (September, 1928), 19.
"From One Generation to Another," *Pictorial Review,* XXX (October, 1928), 20-21.
"The Silver Sword," *Pictorial Review,* XXX (March, 1929), 18-19.
*"Survivor," *Pictorial Review,* XXX (May, 1929), 17-18.
"Pioneers," *Harper's Magazine,* CLIX (July, 1929), 199-210.
"Quicksilver," *Harper's Magazine,* CLIX (August, 1929), 316-30.
"Surprize," *Pictorial Review,* XXX (September, 1929), 16-17.
*"Conjuh," *Pictorial Review,* XXXI (October, 1929), 20-21.
*"In the Shade of the Tree," *Harper's Magazine,* CLX (January, 1930), 153-60.
" 'Ki,' " *Pictorial Review,* XXXI (February, 1930), 16-17.
"Wife of a Viking," *Pictorial Review,* XXXI (April, 1930), 13-14.
*"Can't Cross Jordan by Myself," *Pictorial Review,* XXXI (August, 1930), 10-12.
"Diamond Wedding," *Woman's Home Companion,* LVII (September, 1930), 17-19.
"Green Vigil," *Ladies' Home Journal,* XLVII (September, 1930), 3-5.
"Light," *Ladies' Home Journal,* XLVII (November, 1930), 18-19.
"The Hills of Heaven," *Good Housekeeping,* XCII (January, 1931), 20-23.
*"Renegade," *Ladies' Home Journal,* XLVIII (February, 1931), 8.
*"The Body of the Crime," *Ladies' Home Journal,* XLVIII (March, 1931), 12-13.

"Daughter of the Soil," *Pictorial Review,* XXXII (March, 1931-), 18-19.
*"Man Without a God" ["Man and Boy"], *Ladies' Home Journal,* XLVIII (November–December, 1931), 3-5, 16-17.
*"Conscience" ["Two Seconds"], *Pictorial Review,* XXXIII (January, 1932), 16-17.
"Twenty-seven Minutes," *Ladies' Home Journal,* XLIX (April, 1932), 10-11.
*"By Appointment," *Saturday Evening Post,* CCV (July, 2, 1932), 5-7.
*"How Beautiful with Shoes," *Harper's Magazine,* CLXV (August, 1932), 341-54.
"Where There's Smoke," *Ladies' Home Journal,* XLIX (October, 1932), 14-15.
"Will and Bill," *Ladies' Home Journal,* L (January, 1933), 14-15.
"Somebody," *Harper's Bazaar* (November, 1933), pp. 56-104.
"Landfall," *Liberty,* XII (January, 12, 1935), 20-27.
"Son of His Father," *Saturday Evening Post,* CCVIII (October 12, 1935), 12-13.
"The Second Mrs. Brown," *Collier's Weekly,* XCIX (February 6, 1937), 14-15.
*"Due North," *Cosmopolitan* (June, 1937), pp. 58-130.
*"The Black Road," *Collier's Weekly,* CIII (June 3, 1939), 11-12.
"Baptism," *Good Housekeeping,* CIX (August, 1939), 20-21.
*"Isles of Spice and Lilies," *Atlantic Monthly,* CLXV (February, 1940), 175-80.
"Through Road," *Collier's Weekly,* CV (March 16, 1940), 25.
"A Life Is So Little," *Good Housekeeping,* CXI (October, 1940), 22-23.
"Prescription for Success," *Woman's Home Companion,* LXIX (May, 1942), 18-19.
"Her Hand in Marriage," *Cosmopolitan* (July, 1943), pp. 21-22.
"The Crystal-Gazer's Daughter," *Good Housekeeping,* CXVIII (January, 1944), 38-39.
"The Bogeyman," *The Magazine of Fantasy and Science Fiction,* XV (October, 1958), 99-113.

E. Articles

"Moving-Picture Machine in the Jungle," *McClure's Magazine,* XL (January, 1913), 329-37.
"At the Ocean Crossroads," *Harper's Magazine,* CXXXV (October, 1917), 681-93.
"Beleaguered Island," *Harper's Magazine,* CXXXVI (May, 1918), 817-29.
"Contact," *Harper's Magazine,* CXXXVIII (March, 1919), 485-93.

"Commuters in Barbary," *Harper's Magazine*, CXLIII (July, 1921), 137-50.
"Fourth Pillar," *Harper's Magazine*, CXLIII (August, 1921), 367-79.
"The Mendenine Road," *Harper's Magazine*, CXLIII (October, 1921), 587-601.
"In the Mountains of the Desert," *Harper's Magazine*, CXLIII (November, 1921), 784-97.
"In the Mzab," *Harper's Magazine*, CXLIV (April, 1922), 636-46.

F. Juvenilia

"Third Chronicles," *Kynewisbok*. Denver: University of Denver, 1904, pp. 113-14.
"The Book of Wilbur Daniel, Son of Wilbur, Called The Prowess of '07," *Kynewisbok*. Denver: University of Denver, 1906, pp. 51-52.

SECONDARY SOURCES

BINNEY, CHARLES J. F. *Genealogy of the Binney Family in the United States*. Albany: Joel Munsell's Sons, 1886. Traces Steele's paternal ancestry.
BREIT, HARVEY. "Talk with Mr. Steele," New York *Times*, August 6, 1950, p. 12. Interview focuses on Steele's literary difficulties.
COOK, GEORGE CRAM, and FRANK SHAY, eds. *Provincetown Plays*. Cincinnati: Stewart Kidd Co., 1921. Collection of ten Provincetown plays, including Steele's *Not Smart*.
DEUTSCH, HELEN, and STELLA HANAU. *The Provincetown: A Story of the Theatre*. New York: Farrar & Rinehart, Inc., 1931. Important history; lists all plays and casts.
ELSER, FRANK B. "Oh, Yes . . . Wilbur Daniel Steele," *The Bookman*, LXII (February, 1926), 691-94. Neighborly interview with Steele, his wind-blown personality, nonliterary attitudes, and exacting methods.
GELB, ARTHUR, and BARBARA GELB. *O'Neill*. New York: Harper and Brothers, 1960. Fine discussion of O'Neill and the Provincetown; some references to Steele and O'Neill.
KUNITZ, STANLEY, and HOWARD HAYCROFT. *Twentieth Century Authors*. New York: The H. W. Wilson Company, 1942. Sketches Steele's career and personality.
MIRRIELEES, EDITH R. "The Best of Steele," New York *Times*, July 14, 1946, pp. 5, 20. Reviews *The Best Stories of Wilbur Daniel Steele* and summarizes Steele's tradition, characteristics, and significance.
O'BRIEN, EDWARD J., ed. *Best Short Stories*. Boston: Small, Maynard & Company, 1915–18, 1920–22, 1925; New York: Dodd, Mead

and Company, 1926; Boston: Houghton Mifflin Company, 1933. Reprints of and comments on selected Steele stories.

PETERSON, THEODORE. *Magazines in the Twentieth Century*. Urbana: University of Illinois Press, 1964. Readable history of the American popular magazine, 1900–1964; discusses social and economic forces on magazine industry and editorial policies of magazines containing Steele's stories.

RUGG, WINNIFRED KING. "Wilbur Daniel Steele." Typescript of Interview, Denver Public Library, 1932. Steele's literary opinions in early 1930's (15 pp.).

VORSE, MARY HEATON. *Time and the Town*. New York: Dial Press, 1942. Several anecdotes and references to the young Steele; tells of the Steeles and the Wharf Theater.

WILLIAMS, BLANCHE COLTON, ed., *O. Henry Memorial Prize Stories*. New York: Doubleday, 1919–22, 1924–26, 1928–31. Reprints of and comments on Steele's prize stories.

————*Our Short Story Writers*. New York: Dodd, Mead and Company, 1926. Surveys twenty-two contemporary American story writers. Chapter XXII is devoted to Steele, pp. 372-84.

Index